101 WILDERNESS SURVIVAL TIPS FOR BOYS

101 WILDERNESS SURVIVAL TIPS FOR BOYS

Chris McNab

amber
BOOKS

First published in 2008 by
Amber Books Ltd
Bradley's Close
74–77 White Lion Street
London N1 9PF
United Kingdom
www.amberbooks.co.uk

ISBN 978-1-906626-10-5

Project Editor: Michael Spilling
Design: Graham Beehag
Illustrations: Tony Randell

Printed and bound in Dubai

10 9 8 7 6 5 4 3 2 1

DISCLAIMER
All techniques and practices described in this book should only be carried out under
strict adult supervision and in the safest possible manner. Neither the author or the
publisher can accept responsibility for any loss, injury, or damage caused as a result
of the use of techniques described in this book, nor for any prosecutions
or proceedings brought or instigated against any person or body that may
result from using these techniques.

Contents

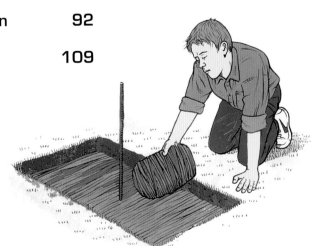

Introduction

We never know when we might need to rely on our survival skills. There are many times and places where we can go from safety to extreme danger in a matter of minutes, such as on a family vacation in the mountains, a school camping trip, or a car journey through desolate wilderness.

That's why it pays to know how to survive in the wild. If you are caught in a life-threatening situation, you are more likely to get through it if you make good decisions and respond properly to the danger. Though there are lots of different survival techniques, the basic principles of survival are very simple. You have to find water and food. Water is especially important, because you can survive with almost no food whatsoever for several weeks, but without water you may die within three days. You also need to be protected from the elements, which usually means building or finding some kind of shelter. You should have some method of making fire, which is important for warmth. Fire also gives you the means to make food and water safe through cooking. Finally, in an emergency you need to know how to attract rescuers or get to safety, and how to look after any injuries you or others may have.

This book brings together some essential survival techniques, including everything from finding water in a dry, hot landscape through to avoiding attack by a bear. Get out there in the woods and practice these techniques—one day, they may save your life.

You will probably have a great time practicing survival techniques, but remember these words of warning. First, if you try any survival techniques that use fire, knives, or hunting weapons, or if you are making traps, make sure that you have a responsible adult with you to supervise. When handling knives, be careful. Always cut <u>away</u> from your body and keep your knife sharp—a blunt knife is actually more dangerous than a sharp one because it is more likely to slip while cutting. And never, ever fool around with a knife! Second, never go out into any wilderness environment alone or without telling an adult exactly where you are going. Always take the right clothing and some food and water.

Once you are in the wild, don't change your plans and go off somewhere else without telling anyone. Third, be careful what you eat. There are many plants and fungi that make wonderful food, but there are also others that can kill you in a matter of hours. Never eat anything that you can't identify as safe to eat. This book will give a quick guide to some common edible plants and how to look out for poisonous ones, but you should arrange for an experienced guide to show you exactly what is safe and what is not.

Finally, don't break the law. Remember, you can't go cutting up trees without the landowner's permission, and carrying knives and hunting weapons may be illegal in some states. Never try to kill any wild animals unless you really have to for survival. However, you can still practice tracking and stalking.

Survival is all about respect for nature and personal toughness. You have to respect nature because, in the end, it is always more powerful than you. And it is more likely to kill you if you give up. History shows that there have been dozens of people who managed to stay alive despite having no survival training because they thought clearly about their actions. And no matter how bad the situation became, they did not surrender to fear and weakness. With the same attitude, but armed with the survival techniques explained here, you are well prepared for the wild.

TIP 1 Essential Equipment

When you have to survive in the wild, having the right kit can mean the difference between life and death. Gather a few simple items in your pack, and you are ready to set out on your adventure.

Whether you are stuck out on a freezing mountainside, or deep within a tropical forest, it will often be your kit that keeps you alive. Pack enough food and water for your trip, including good, high-energy food like dried fruit, nuts, and ricecakes. Take some chocolate bars and sweets, but not too many—they provide only short bursts of energy that wear off quickly. Now think about your survival kit. Make sure you have the following:

1) a good flashlight and plenty of spare batteries;
2) a pair of binoculars;
3) a sleeping bag—wrapped in a waterproof bag;
4) a whistle—to signal for help;
5) a small pocketknife;
6) a map of the area you're heading into;
7) washing kit—soap, washcloth, toothbrush, toothpaste; and
8) a mess tin—a metal tin in which you can cook food.

If you have all these items, plus those in your survival tin (see Tip 3), you will be well prepared to survive if disaster strikes.

TRUE LIFE SURVIVAL !

Not packing the right equipment and food can have terrible consequences, as the British explorer Robert Falcon Scott discovered. In 1910, Scott and a four-man team began a journey to reach the South Pole in Antarctica. They were racing against a Norwegian team to be the first to reach the Pole, but when they arrived on January 17–18, 1912, they found the Norwegian flag already planted there. They now had to make the horrible return journey through freezing blizzards. At this point, the men were all suffering from scurvy, a disease that is the result of not eating enough vitamin C. This is found in fruit such as lemons and oranges, but Scott had not packed any fruit or vegetables. The scurvy meant that all the men became weak and were unable to keep going. Just a few pieces of fruit would have cured them. One by one, they died, from malnutrition, from frostbite, and by freezing.

TIP 2

Make a Horseshoe Pack

Stuck in the wilderness and don't have a backpack? Don't worry—you can make a horseshoe pack in minutes! Here's a really great way to carry all your survival items into the wild.

To begin, find a large, square piece of material such as a poncho, tent canvas, or blanket. You'll also need a long piece of string. Now lay the material on the floor and place all the items that you need to carry along one edge. Make sure that you spread the items out evenly along the length of the blanket. Now start rolling up the blanket with all the items inside the material—work from the side where the objects are, and carry on rolling until you reach the opposite edge. You'll end up with a long tube of fabric. Snip off two pieces of string and tie off the ends of the roll to keep all the items trapped inside. Then tie two more pieces of string at evenly spaced intervals around the middle of the roll—these will stop the items from slipping around inside the tube. You're nearly done. All you need to do now is now tie the two ends together, throw the pack over your shoulder, and set off on your travels!

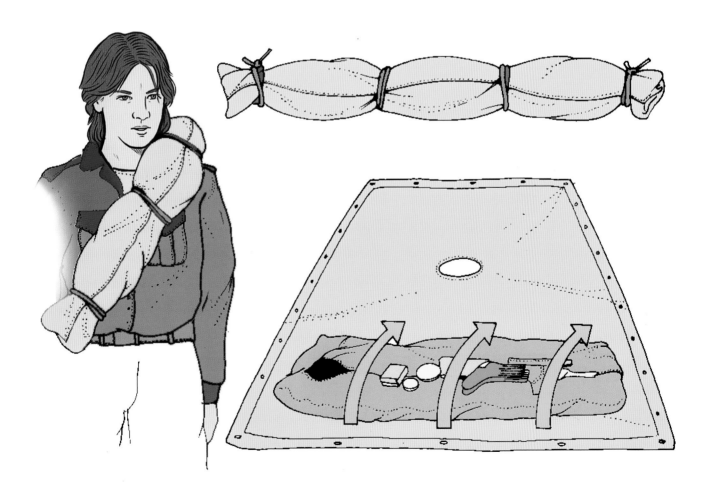

Prepare a Survival Tin

A survival tin is a whole survival kit that can fit into one pocket! Every time you venture out into the wilderness, even if it's only for a few hours, take your survival tin.

You are stuck in the wilderness with no food, water or shelter…but if you have a survival tin, your chances of survival are much greater. Here's how to make one. First find a small tin or plastic box with a snug, watertight lid (tobacco tins or sturdy plastic food containers are good). Now buy or find the following items, and pack them carefully inside the tin:

1) a book of matches—dip the match heads in melted candle wax and let it dry to make the matches waterproof. Just scrape off the wax to use them;
2) a small candle;
3) a flint and striker for starting fires—you can buy these from any camping gear supplier;
4) a sewing kit for repairing damaged clothing;
5) signaling mirror;
6) fishing hooks, line, and weights;
7) a coil of thin brass wire for making snares;
8) a week's supply of water purification tables;
9) safety pins;
10) a small button compass; and
11) a coiled-up wire saw.

With this kit in your pocket, you are ready for anything! You can make fires, catch food, drink clean water, build shelters, and repair your clothes.

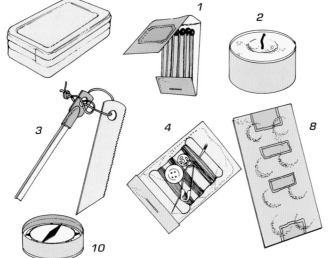

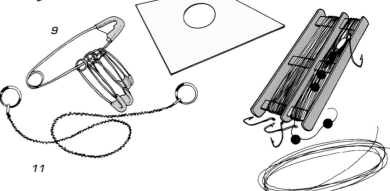

TIP 4

Finding Water in the Landscape

You can live for up to two weeks without food, but without water you'll be dead in two or three days. Don't panic! Even if the sun is blazing, there is water to be found in the hills, valleys, and woods around you.

TRUE LIFE SURVIVAL !

When Danelle Ballengee went for a run in the wilderness around Moab, Utah, with his dog Taz in December 2006, he had no idea that he would shortly be fighting for his life. While running along a canyon, he slipped on some ice and fell 20ft (6m), smashing his pelvis in half. (The pelvis is the large bone that holds the hips and legs in place.) It was an injury that could have killed him, but despite horrible pain he knew he had to get out of the canyon. He began to crawl using his arms alone, an exhausting process. He became dehydrated, so he drank from pools of meltwater that he found among the rocks. By drinking this fluid, and keeping warm by doing stomach crunch exercises, he stayed alive and awake for 52 hours. Eventually Taz ran off and alerted rescuers out looking for Danelle—the dog actually led the rescuers back to Danelle and he was taken to a hospital and safety.

If you are lost in the wild and have no water, time is running out. The landscape may look completely dry, but with some expert skills you'll be able to track down life-saving fluids. The most important rule is that water runs from high ground to low ground, and it likes to follow channels. Go exploring—search in the bottoms of valleys or in gullies for hidden streams, and look closely at rockfaces to see if there is water trickling out of cracks. Shaded rocky areas may have water trapped in little pools. Look also at plants and animals. Do you see green, lush plants in a dry wilderness? That often means there is water nearby, even if it is underground (see "Dig for Water," Tip 5). Grazing animals like cows and deer will often amble off for water at dusk—following them could lead you to a stream, but don't track them so far that you lose your way and get lost. Insects like to stay around water, so look for clouds of flies buzzing over certain patches of land. Also, watch out for ants marching straight up a tree—they may have found water trapped in a hole in the trunk.

When a river dries up, the inside bends of the rivers are often the last places to lose their surface water. That's why they are great places to look for water in an emergency.

11

TIP 5 — Dig for Water

You've hunted for water on the land, and found nothing. The situation is looking desperate. The answer could be just beneath your feet.

Water may disappear quickly from the surface of the land, but it could still be underground. Here are some good places you should explore:

1) Seemingly dried-up riverbeds. In particular, look around the outside edge of bends, shaded or rocky areas, or deep holes.

2) The trough between two sand dunes or irrigation trenches (trenches used to carry water into fields).

3) Just above the high tide mark on a beach— you'll see this by a line of debris on the sand.

Once you've found a promising spot, it's time to start digging! Find a large branch and, using a knife, carve off shavings of wood from one end until you have a flat edge like a spade. Then use the stick to chop straight down into the earth, creating a hole about 1ft (30cm) across.

After a while, the soil may get damp and the hole start to fill with water seeping through the sides. Collect any pools of water in a cup, filter it and boil it to drink. If your digging finds nothing but dry earth after you've dug several feet down, move somewhere else.

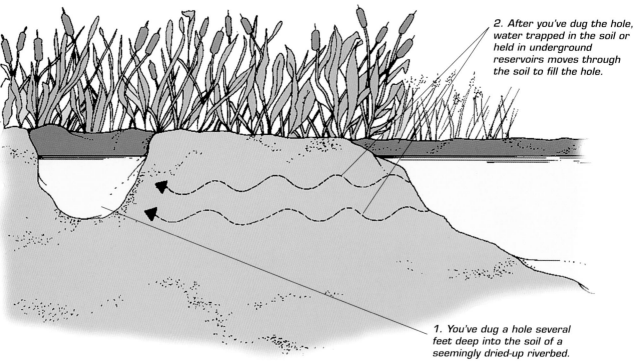

2. After you've dug the hole, water trapped in the soil or held in underground reservoirs moves through the soil to fill the hole.

1. You've dug a hole several feet deep into the soil of a seemingly dried-up riverbed.

TIP 6

Make a Water Filter

You've collected a nice cup of water from a stream or river…. Don't drink it! The water might look clean, but it could contain a lot of bacteria and bugs, and the last thing you need is to make yourself sick.

The first thing you have to do with survival water is remove all the dirt. One of the simplest methods is to pour the water through a piece of close-woven fabric (like an old T-shirt) and let it drain into a container (see illustration below). Do this several times—you'll see dirt collecting on the fabric (dirt that you would have drunk if you hadn't filtered the water). Even better, make a filter system. The best filters use several layers of different materials. Make a good improvised filter by first creating a cloth bag (such as a T-shirt with the neck and sleeves tied off), and filling this with alternate layers of material. This could be a layer of sand, then one of rocks, another of sand, another of rocks. Pour the water into the top of the bag and let it drain through to drip into a container below. Each layer will take out a different type of dirt from the water. You could also make a filter frame. This is like a tipi with open bags suspended between the arms, each bag containing a filtering material—see the illustration below. Once you have filtered the water, purify it before drinking.

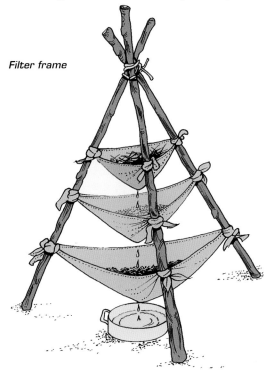

Filter frame

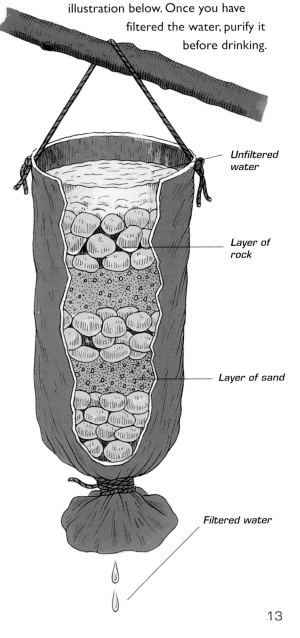

Unfiltered water

Layer of rock

Layer of sand

Filtered water

TIP 7

Make Rain Traps

It may not seem like it, but rain can be your best friend in the wild. So when the dark clouds gather, get ready with your rain traps...

The great thing about rainwater is that it's clean and safe to drink. That's why when it rains you should collect as much as possible by using rain traps. Make a simple rain trap by wrapping a long cloth around the trunk of a tree, with the loose end at the bottom positioned over a container. When it rains, the cloth gets soaked with water running down the trunk, and this then drips into the container. This water is usually safe to gulp down right away. Or, tie a waterproof sheet (such as a tent groundsheet) between four poles stuck in the ground, and use some stones to make the sheet dip at one end—put a container beneath the edge where it dips. When it rains, the water will run down the cloth, past the stones and into the

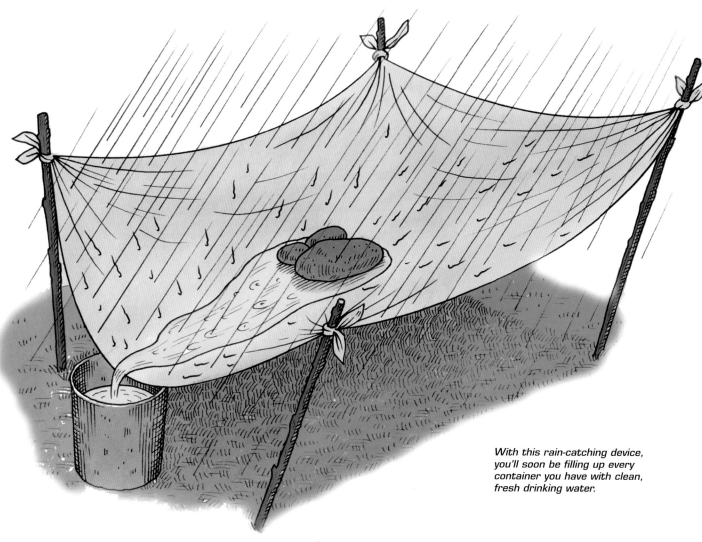

With this rain-catching device, you'll soon be filling up every container you have with clean, fresh drinking water.

container. If you are fit enough, another good way to collect lots of rainwater is to dig a large circular pit and line it with plastic. When it rains, the water fills up the pit, and you'll soon have your own personal reservoir! Remember, don't leave any rainwater for too long before drinking it—it will go stagnant in a few days.

TRUE LIFE SURVIVAL !

Rainwater has been all that separates many survivors from death. One of the most incredible survival stories ever occurred in 2001 in the Pacific Ocean. Four fishermen from the island of Samoa had to abandon their fishing boat in June that year when it began to topple over under the weight of a heavy load of fish. They got into a small aluminum dinghy, and then floated alone in the Pacific for nearly five months. Two of the men died in the boat, but the other two survived for 132 days at sea by catching rainwater and eating any fish they caught. Their boat was finally spotted off the coast of Papua New Guinea—more than 2,500 miles (4,000km) from home—and they were rescued.

Plastic groundsheet

Stone weights

TIP 8 Purify Water

You are feeling sick and dizzy. Your stomach is rumbling, and you feel the urge to rush to the toilet. The reason could be that cup of water you drank just half an hour ago…

Even if you filter water, it may still contain invisible bacteria. These can be poisonous and may even kill you—and that's why you need to purify water. It's not difficult. The two best, and quickest, ways to purify water are by using professional kits. Purification tablets are cheap to buy and easy to carry. They are chemicals that kill bacteria, and you simply follow the instructions carefully on the packet to make water safe to drink. Another way is to use a water purification pump. You can buy one of these from an adventure sports supplier. The pump contains the purification chemicals inside, so all you do is put one end of the pump in the water, pump the handle up and down, and clean drinking water will come instantly out of the pump's pipe. It's that easy! Yet there is a natural method of purification that's just as good. Simply put a metal container of filtered water over a fire and bring the water to a boil. Boil it for 10 minutes, then allow it to cool. It's now safe to drink. One word of warning, however. If the water has any manmade chemicals in it, such as fertilizer, even boiling won't make it safe to drink.

Pot for boiling water. The cloth over the top stops you losing lots of precious water as steam.

16

TIP 9

Make a Solar Still

Lost in a scorching desert, with nothing surrounding you but hot sand and rock, you'll soon be desperate for water. Here's how nothing but a few plastic bags can save your life…

There are many places in the world, particularly deserts, where there is almost no water and it rarely rains. How is it possible to stay alive in these conditions? Don't panic…there is one way to make small quantities of perfectly safe drinking water. Water vapor consists of small particles of water in the air—and it can be a life saver! You can trap the vapor by making what is called a "solar still." First you need a large sheet of plastic (or open out a plastic bag). Make sure the plastic has no holes in it. Then dig a hole in the ground about 1ft (30cm) deep and place a container in the bottom. The hole must be a few inches narrower than the plastic sheet. Stretch the sheet over the hole and weigh it down around the edge with rocks and soil—don't leave any gaps, or the baking sun will cook off any water vapor. Then place a single stone in the middle of the plastic so that it sags down over the container. Now leave for a full day. The heat of the daytime will make water vapor rise out of the soil and then turn into condensation on the underside of the plastic. This condensation then runs down the plastic and drips into the container. With a few of these stills on the go, you can keep yourself alive.

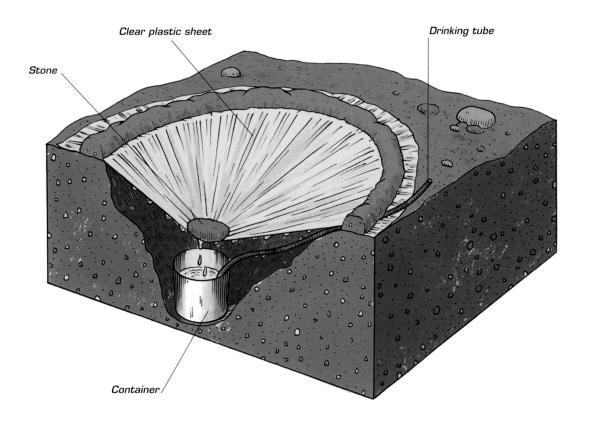

Stone

Clear plastic sheet

Drinking tube

Container

TIP 10 Make a Vegetation Still

In a forest-covered wilderness, the trees and bushes won't just give you food. With this expert technique, they will also give you water.

Here's how to make a "vegetation still." Find a plastic bag. Make sure that it doesn't have the little holes or tears in it—any holes at all will stop the device from working. Now find a green and bushy piece of foliage, and put the bag over it. Don't use dry, dead foliage—it won't give out any water. Tie the neck of the bag securely against the branch, and don't leave any gaps. Now leave it for 24 hours. The air inside the bag warms up and draws water vapor out of the foliage. This vapor then condenses into water droplets on the inside of the bag, which then run down and collect at the bottom of the bag, ready to drink. When you put the bag onto the tree or bush, try to leave room between the bag and the branches and leaves, otherwise the plant might simply soak up the droplets. You can position one or two bare twigs to push the plastic away from the foliage. As with the solar still, you may need several vegetation stills to make life-saving amounts of water.

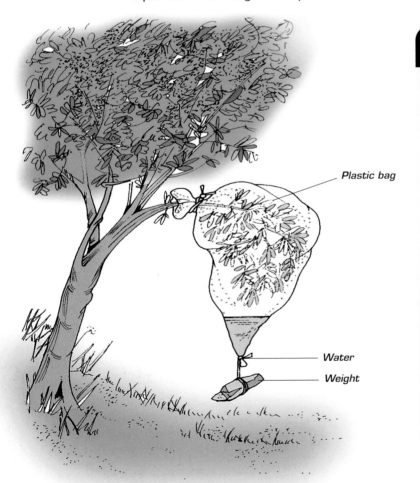

Plastic bag

Water

Weight

TRUE LIFE SURVIVAL !

Want more proof that stills can be true life savers? In January 1982, Steven Callahan found himself adrift at sea in a life raft after his boat sank near the Canary Islands (a group of islands off the coast of northwest Africa). He had only 8 pints (4.5 liters) of water, but he also had a solar still with him, one designed to make saltwater drinkable. (Saltwater in the bottom of the still evaporates, leaving the salt behind, then condenses on the dome of the still and runs down as fresh water into a collection bottle.) He came close to death several times, and had to fight off sharks constantly. Yet even though he was adrift for 76 days before rescue, the solar still meant that he could provide himself with just enough drinking water to stay alive.

TIP 11 How to Choose a Campsite

Choosing the wrong place to make your camp could mean disaster—everything from being bitten to death by insects to being crushed by falling trees.

Rule number one: don't make camp on top of a hill, where wind and rain will batter you. It's much better to find a position where rocks, hills, or trees shelter you from the worst of the wind, though in warm climates you do want a hint of a breeze to carry away smoke and insects. However, don't make a shelter in a valley bottom or hollow ground—these can be extremely cold and damp at night, or could fill with water if it rains. Instead, select a sheltered spot on flat, dry ground. Make sure that plenty of wood (for making fire) and a river or stream (for water and fishing) are nearby because you don't want to be walking miles for essentials. Your campsite should be far enough from a waterway so that you aren't flooded if the water levels suddenly rise. Now look up—don't build a shelter or pitch a tent under old, dead-looking trees because large boughs could break off and crush you. Check too that there are no wasp, hornet, bee, or ant nests nearby—an insect attack is the last thing you need when trying to survive!

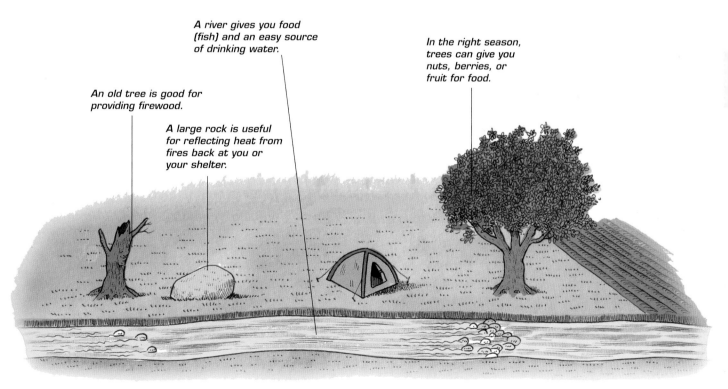

A river gives you food (fish) and an easy source of drinking water.

In the right season, trees can give you nuts, berries, or fruit for food.

An old tree is good for providing firewood.

A large rock is useful for reflecting heat from fires back at you or your shelter.

TIP 12 — Lay Out a Camp Properly

A roaring log fire, a warm and comfortable shelter, food and water stored nearby…you've just built the perfect survival camp.

If you are lost in the wilderness, don't allow yourself to sink into despair. Instead, throw yourself into making a great camp. First, clear a circular patch of ground about 10ft (3m) in diameter—just use a leafy bough to sweep the ground clear of leaves, grasses, and twigs. Place your fire in the middle, and build your shelter on the edge. This way, your shelter and the surroundings won't be in danger of catching fire from sparks or flames. It's also a good idea to build your fire near a large rock or tree stump. When the fire is blazing, the rock will reflect heat onto your back if you sit between it and the fire, keeping you warm all around. Gather kindling and firewood and make a pile of it within easy reach. Also build a rain trap nearby, so you can catch rain while you are asleep. If you are in a rainy part of the world, it can be a good idea to cut a gutter into the soil around your shelter to deflect water away from the camp if there is a sudden downpour. Finally, build a latrine about 328ft (100m) away from the camp. Make sure that it is downwind so that unpleasant odors don't waft back toward you.

10ft (3m) clearing

Building your fire on a good clear patch of ground means your shelter and the surrounding forest should be safe from the flames.

TRUE LIFE SURVIVAL

A camp can be very basic, but when the weather is bad it is essential. In September 2007 Russian adventurer Aleksandr Zverev went white-water rafting along a raging river in western China. In two separate accidents, four of the party were killed when the rafts overturned, and Aleksandr was left alone in the Chinese wilderness with no food or water. He was wearing only pants, a T-shirt and a hooded raincoat, and the climate was often cold and wet. He used caves along the riverbank for shelter and every night he made a bed for himself out of tree branches. By keeping warm as best he could, and by drinking river water, he survived in the wild for 25 days before being rescued.

Make a Tree Shelter

Snow is falling thick and fast. You are wet and cold. What you need is a quick, easy shelter to stop you from freezing to death.

Tree shelters are a great way to get out of the wind and the wet. All you need is one fir tree and some branches. Find a good, bushy fir tree and scrape a trench around its base, deep enough for you to sit in. What happens is that the thick canopy of branches above your head actually forms a roof above you, which keeps out the rain and wind. Stacking up rocks around the perimeter of your hole also helps keep the wind away. If you plan to use the shelter for any length of time, you can improve on it by propping up branches against the trunk of the

tree from the edge of the hole, all the way around. Strengthen this structure by interlocking the branches at the trunk, or tying them around the trunk with a piece of cord. Cover the branches with thick layers of foliage, and the shelter is done!

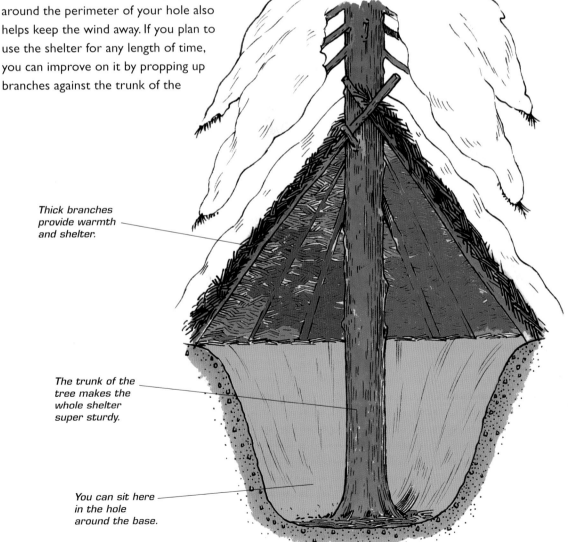

Thick branches provide warmth and shelter.

The trunk of the tree makes the whole shelter super sturdy.

You can sit here in the hole around the base.

TIP 14 Make a Snow Shelter

When stuck out for the night in a snowy wilderness without shelter, or when faced with a raging blizzard, a snow shelter could save your life.

The easiest type of snow shelter is the snow cave. Find a deep snowdrift that is made up of thick, fairly hard snow. Now dig straight into the deep part of the drift about 3ft (1m), making the hole big enough for you to crawl through. Once inside, widen the end of the hole out into a living quarters, big enough for you to sit comfortably. Make sure the ceiling and walls are a dome shape. That way, any meltwater will run down the sides and not drip onto your head. Line the floor with lots of branches—fir tree branches are good—so that you have something warm and dry to sit on. Then, using a stick, bore two small holes through the wall of the cave to provide ventilation. (This is a very important step, so don't leave it out!) Use your backpack or a tied bundle of foliage as a "door." Another way to form a snow shelter is to make a large pile of twigs and foliage, pile snow thickly over it, let the snow harden, then carefully pull out the branches to leave a hollow cave something like an igloo.

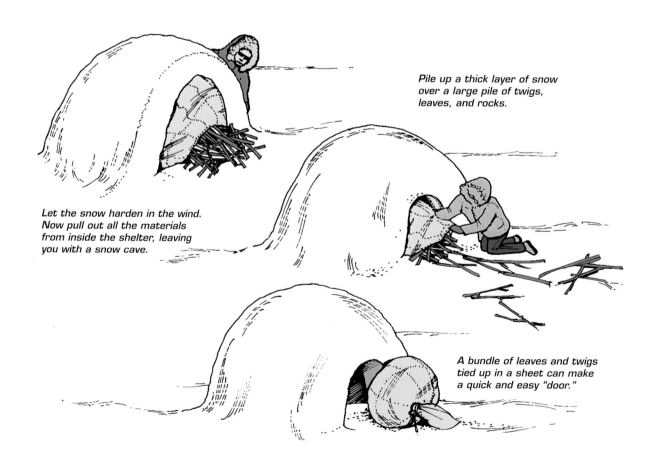

Pile up a thick layer of snow over a large pile of twigs, leaves, and rocks.

Let the snow harden in the wind. Now pull out all the materials from inside the shelter, leaving you with a snow cave.

A bundle of leaves and twigs tied up in a sheet can make a quick and easy "door."

（）

In a snow cave, make a separate bed area, lined with a thick layer of fir branches. This should be higher than the rest of the shelter to catch the rising warmer air.

TRUE LIFE SURVIVAL

In 1995 Andrew Wilson, a 44-year-old skier, was skiing with a friend in the Scottish Highlands when a terrifying blizzard descended. The blizzard produced a "white out"—snow so thick that you can't see even a few feet in front of you—and he became completely disoriented. Wilson was separated from his friend, and in wind-chill temperatures of -22°F (-30°C) he quickly became locked in a fight for his survival. He would be stuck out on the mountain for three days and nights. He was an experienced outdoorsman, however, and burrowed out a snow cave in a thick snow drift, where he sat out the worst of the storm in his sleeping bag. He was finally spotted by a rescue helicopter—his survival skills had kept him alive long enough for rescue.

A bird's-eye view of a snow cave. Don't forget the ventilation holes—you could suffocate without them!

Ventilation hole

Door

Sleeping platform

Bed of leaves

TIP 15 Make a Lean-to Shelter

In survival, a forest is your friend! As long as there are branches around you, you will never be without shelter.

Building a lean-to shelter shows that you are becoming a real survival expert! To begin, first make a frame out of strong, large branches stripped of their foliage. The frame can be as simple as a large branch propped horizontally between two trees (or other features), with other branches laid vertically against it. (Make sure that the slope of the frame is facing into the wind.) Alternatively, you may not need to make a horizontal support at all—simply prop the vertical branches against, say, a partially fallen tree or a rock face. Ideally, use some cord or thick, flexible plants to tie the frame securely together. Find bushy branches (fir tree branches are really good) and lay these against the frame to form a thick, warm, and almost waterproof covering. Interlock the branches to make this covering more stable, and pack any gaps with mud and soil. As with any shelter, cover the ground inside it with more thick layers of foliage—you will lose too much body heat if you sit on bare ground.

! TRUE LIFE SURVIVAL

To see the power of a simple shelter, just consider the story of Jacob Allen. In October 2007, he wandered away from his parents in the Monongahela National Forest. Allen is autistic, and though he was 18 years old at the time, he has a much lower mental age. He became lost, and the weather closed in, bringing freezing nighttime temperatures. Eventually his fearful parents alerted the authorities, and a major rescue effort began. He was not discovered for four days—but he was found alive. Allen had survived by hiding under a mass of laurel and rhododendron plants hanging from rocks. The foliage was so thick that it protected him from the wet and the wind like an umbrella. His experience shows how even natural shelters can have a major impact on your chances of survival in the wild.

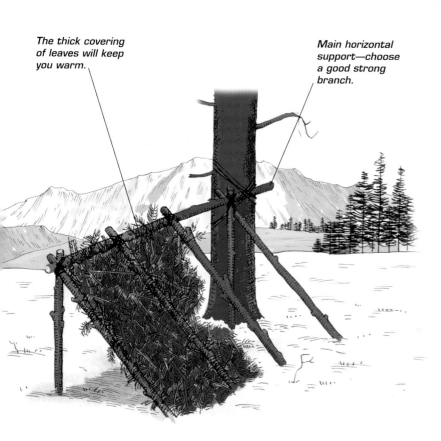

The thick covering of leaves will keep you warm.

Main horizontal support—choose a good strong branch.

TIP
16

Make a Tipi

There is nothing quite as cozy as being tucked up inside a tipi. Take a tip from the Native American people by learning to make this simple but effective shelter.

The best thing about a tipi is that you can pack it up and take it from place to place, saving you time and energy. Properly made, tipis are sturdy and well ventilated, and if constructed from the right materials they also allow a fire to be made inside. However, a survival tipi is a little rougher—under no circumstances should you make a fire inside this structure. First, you need some poles. Cut about five or six long, straight branches down to roughly the same length—about 6ft (1.8m). Draw a circle on the ground with a stick, then place the thick base of each branch at equal intervals around the circle. Dig small holes for the branches to sit in, then one by one tie the top ends together with cord or flexible plants to form the classic tipi shape. Now wrap the frame in a large, waterproof sheet—such as a groundsheet—and tie the sheet together at several points down

the "opening" to enclose the space. Or, cover the frame with thick layers of foliage, remembering to leave a gap as a door you can crawl through. This improvised tipii is only big enough to sit in, but once inside you'll feel warm and protected.

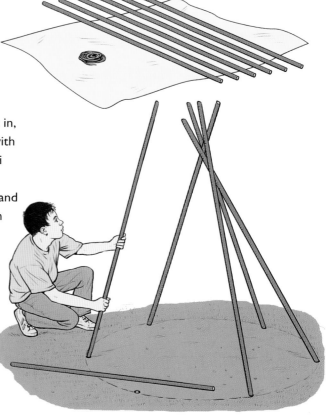

All you need for a basic tipi are some poles, a sheet of material, and some cord. See how the boy here has marked a circle on the ground to help him place the poles correctly. Now he ties the top of the poles together and covers the structure with the sheet to produce a quick, solid shelter.

TIP 17 — Make an A-frame Shelter

You need somewhere safe to sleep at night, a place that will protect you from rain, wind, and roaming animals.

An A-frame shelter is ideal nighttime shelter for sleeping in, because it can be long enough for the whole body. First you need a long, straight branch fixed horizontally at least 4ft (1.2m) above the ground (let's call this the "support branch"). You can make this by either sitting the branch on two Y-shaped supports at each end (make these from the forks of large branches) or jamming it between two solid features, like two trees that are growing near each other. Once you have done this, lay other branches at an angle from the ground to the support branch, working from both sides. Interlock them at the top and tie them in place. If you have some rope, you could tie other horizontal branches across the frame as shown in the picture here, making it very strong. Once you have your frame, cover it in a thick layer of branches, leaves, grass, earth, and mud. An even quicker A-frame shelter can be made by propping just one end of the support branch against the fork of a tree, a tall rock, or a fallen tree trunk. This shelter might slope downward, but your feet can go at the low end when you are sleeping.

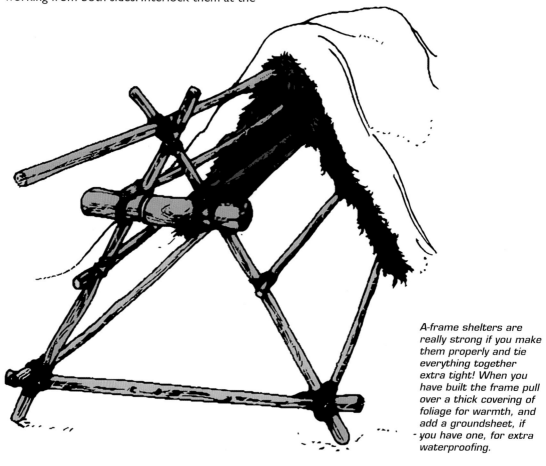

A-frame shelters are really strong if you make them properly and tie everything together extra tight! When you have built the frame pull over a thick covering of foliage for warmth, and add a groundsheet, if you have one, for extra waterproofing.

In hot climates you don't even need a door—just something to protect you from sun and rain.

TRUE LIFE SURVIVAL !

Survival shelters aren't always what you expect. In November 2006, Daryl Blake Jane was trapped in his SUV on a remote snowbound road near Mount Adams in Washington state. The weather conditions were terrible. The snow piled up into drifts 7ft (2.1m) high and pulled over entire trees under its weight. All traffic along the 57-mile (91-km) road had stopped. The only food Jane had in the car was some banana chips, rice cakes, and a little water, which he rationed out for the days ahead. Inside the car, the temperature plunged to well below zero, though he occasionally ran the engine to generate some heat. He sometimes had to exit the car to clear away snow threatening to bury him. By using his car as a shelter, however, he survived for two weeks until found by a snowmobile rescue patrol.

The leaves overlap one another to make any rainwater run off downward.

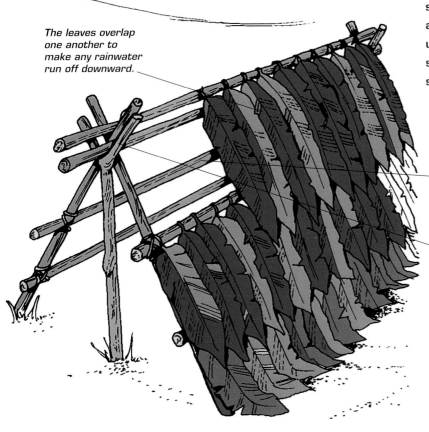

Support branches

Y-shaped support

Make a Hammock

Curled up inside a gently swaying hammock, your campfire smoking nearby, you might forget that this is about survival.

Hammocks can be really comfortable survival beds, so long as you have the right materials to put one together. You will need a large sheet of strong fabric, longer than your own body. Lay the sheet out flat, fold it in half, then mark the center point at the top and the bottom. Next, go to one end and fold up the material from both sides in 2-in (5-cm) deep folds, as if you were making a paper fan, with the folds meeting in the middle. Then tie your supporting rope around the end several inches below the center mark. Fold over the concertina-ed material above the supporting rope knot and tie that firmly in place below the knot. This will prevent the knot from slipping out. Repeat this process at the other end, and you can then tie up your hammock between two trees. Another simple hammock, seen here, involves rolling up two strong branches in the ends of the fabric, then tying ropes from the branches to tree supports. Hammocks are more suited to hot weather climates than cold zones, because they don't give you much warmth from underneath. So don't put up a hammock when snow is falling!

This tropical hammock is simply strung between three trees. It makes a great bed for hot climates because it is cool to sleep on and it is well away from all the insects on the ground beneath.

TIP 19 Make an Improvised Bed

The cold ground will suck the heat from your body if you lie down on it. That's why a survival bed is never a luxury.

A survival bed does two things. First, it helps you get a better night's sleep, and that means you are better able to fight off sickness and keep your spirits up. Second, lying on bare ground is a good way to get infested with insects (in hot climates) or to lose body heat into the ground (in cold climates). The simplest bed is made of thick layers of foliage laid on the ground to provide padding and insulation. Good materials for this are lots of grasses and ferns and also fir-tree branches. Fir branches are really good because they lie flat and keep their needles even during the winter. Pile these materials up in a thick layer and then, if you have it, cover them with a sheet to make a quick bed. In hot climates, it's best to make your bed off the ground, otherwise the bugs will eat you for dinner! Make a platform of poles several inches from the ground—see the illustrations for how to do this—then make your bed on the platform.

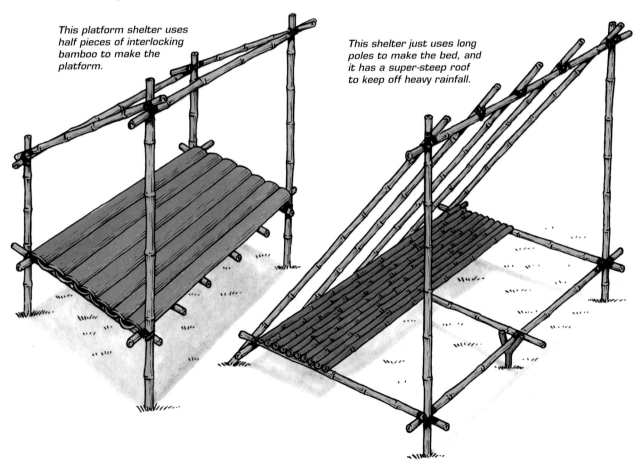

This platform shelter uses half pieces of interlocking bamboo to make the platform.

This shelter just uses long poles to make the bed, and it has a super-steep roof to keep off heavy rainfall.

TIP 20

Make an Animal Alarm

It's nighttime and there's a worrying rustle in the bushes. It could be the wind, or it could be a grizzly bear about to raid your camp.

Many wild animals will not hesitate to sneak into your camp and steal your food. Bears, cougars, and wolves are just some of the dangers. Keep your camp as clean as possible to avoid attracting such creatures, and don't store your food inside your own tent or shelter— you don't want to wake up with a hungry bear looming over you! A good way to store food safely is to keep it in containers or bags hung from a high line suspended between two trees. An extra precaution you can make is an animal alarm. This is designed to alert you at night if an animal heads into your camp. Tie tin cans at intervals along a long piece of string and put stones inside each can. Then tie that string between bushes and trees on the perimeter of your camp, low enough to be snagged by an

animal walking along. If you don't have any string, simply hang the cans on branches and then pull the branches across any tracks or natural entry points into your camp. An animal brushing past the alarm should set the cans rattling and tell you that you have an intruder. (It will also tell you if people are approaching!)

TRUE LIFE SURVIVAL

Wolves generally leave people alone, but on rare occasions they can be a real danger. In February 1915, a team from the Canadian Arctic Expedition made camp in the Northwest Territories of Canada. While the men were in their tents, their sled dogs were curled up outside. Suddenly they heard the sound of dogs fighting outside, and emerged to find a large female wolf attacking the sled dogs. One of the men ran at the wolf, attempting to scare it off, but instead the wolf attacked him. Another man called Jenness managed to grab the wolf by the scruff of the neck, but the wolf twisted around and bit him hard on the arm. Jenness fought back, however, and managed to half strangle the wolf. Eventually the wolf ran away, and was shot by one of the other men of the party.

TIP 21

Make a Latrine

To survive, you have to stay healthy. Making a latrine might not sound interesting, but it's important if you want to keep disease away.

A good latrine will help keep illness, insects, and some animals away from your main living and eating areas. (Amazingly, bears are actually attracted to the smell of human waste.) It should be one of the first things you make if you plan to stay in your camp for more than a day. Choose the right site—at least 328ft (100m) away from your camp area. Make sure it is not too far away—you don't want to get lost looking for the toilet in a blizzard! Also make the latrine behind some bushes or other

feature, so you have a little privacy. Position it downwind from you: that means the wind hits you first, then the latrine. If you do it the other way around, some pretty horrible odors will blow back into your camp. Once you have a location, dig a trench about 2ft (0.6m) deep, 3ft (1m) long, and 1 ft (0.3m) wide. You use the latrine by squatting over the trench with one foot on each side. Each time you use the latrine, cover your excrement with a thick sprinkling of earth.

TIP 22 Protect Yourself Against Insects

Don't worry too much about bears, snakes, and big cats. In the wild, your real enemy can be clouds of biting and stinging insects.

Insects can be a real curse. Not only can they bite and sting, but they also spread disease. Particularly in warm climates, you won't be able to avoid them, but there are ways to reduce the number that bother you. First, make sure you pack insect repellent—plaster this over all parts of your body, including the hands, face, and neck. Keep as much of your body covered with clothing as possible. This is really important for your legs, because your boots and pants will protect you from ticks, chiggers, and ants, which can attach themselves to you from ground foliage. Insects generally don't like smoke, so a good smoky fire can keep down the insects around your camp. In areas with lots of aggressive insect types—particularly the tropics—a piece of thin netting worn over your head and tucked into your shirt collar can help protect you from night attacks. If you find yourself in a sudden swarm of bees or wasps, keep your mouth shut tightly, cover your head and body, and stay still until the swarm passes. If it attacks you, try to run through thick foliage— the branches and leaves will break up the insects' flight paths.

This person is wearing full insect protection. All parts of the body are covered, and look at the elastic bands around the shirt cuffs and ankles. These will stop stinging and biting insects from wriggling their way inside the clothing.

TIP 23 Fell a Tree

Need some serious wood for a shelter or fire? Here's how you can cut down a tree and become a survival lumberjack.

Cutting down a small tree with an axe or saw is an exhausting business, and should be attempted only if it is necessary and safe to do so. First you need the right tools. This really means a professional axe, machete (for small trees), or saw, but in a survival situation you might have to improvise. If you have a wire saw in your survival tin, you can tie this to pieces of wood as shown here to make a hand saw, though this is only suitable for small trees. Now work out where you want the tree to fall (the landing area should be clear and have the wind blowing behind it). The first cuts need to be on the side the tree will fall. Cut a notch halfway through the trunk, with the top of the notch at an angle of 45°. If the tree starts pinching the

axe or saw, widen the notch a little with a new cut. Once you are halfway through, cut another notch in from the other side. This notch should end just higher than the first notch, leaving a "hinge" of wood between the two. The hinge is vital, because it stops the tree trunk from bouncing backward at you when the tree falls. As you finish this cut, the tree should start to topple. Once it begins to move, run off to the side, not directly behind the tree, and let it come crashing down.

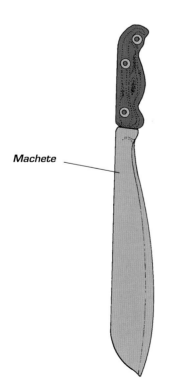

Machete

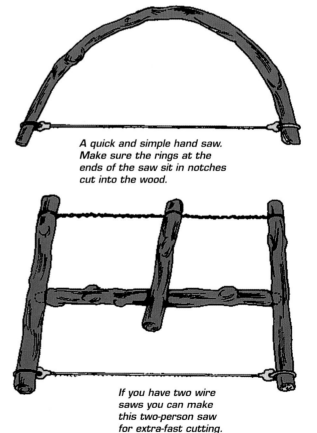

A quick and simple hand saw. Make sure the rings at the ends of the saw sit in notches cut into the wood.

If you have two wire saws you can make this two-person saw for extra-fast cutting.

TIP 24

The Basics of Fire

Even in the most desolate wilderness, a good fire will bring you warmth, light, heat, and cooked food.

Any fire needs four elements—tinder, kindling, fuel, and air. Tinder is used to get the fire started, and can be any light, fibrous material that catches fire easily. In a survival setting, this can include dry straw, leaves, mosses, grasses, the lining of bird or animal nests, and threads of lint or cotton wool. Grind all these up a little between two rocks to open up the fibers. Tinder needs to be bone dry to ignite, so keep it warm and away from the damp. You need a pile of tinder about the size of two fists to make your fire. Kindling is what you add to the tinder once it is lit to make the fire hotter so

you can then add fuel. The best kindling is pencil-thin dry sticks. (Choose brown sticks because young, green sticks don't burn very well.) Other types of kindling can include pine cones and pieces of bark. Once the kindling has raised the fire to a good blaze, add your fuel— large pieces of dry wood or, in an emergency, dry animal dung. (You can use damp wood if you want to make lots of smoke for signaling purposes.) Remember, fire needs air to keep going, so when you are lighting your fuel don't pile on your materials too thickly, or you might smother the blaze.

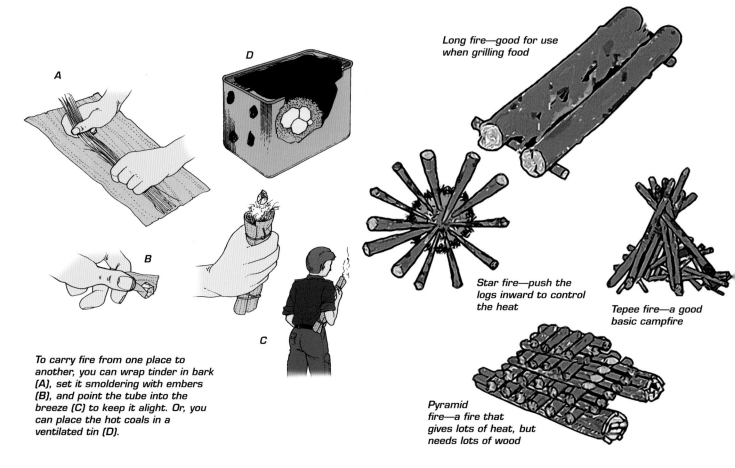

Long fire—good for use when grilling food

Star fire—push the logs inward to control the heat

Tepee fire—a good basic campfire

Pyramid fire—a fire that gives lots of heat, but needs lots of wood

To carry fire from one place to another, you can wrap tinder in bark (A), set it smoldering with embers (B), and point the tube into the breeze (C) to keep it alight. Or, you can place the hot coals in a ventilated tin (D).

TIP 25 Make a Fire with a Friction Bow

Don't have any matches? Don't worry! People have been making fire with the friction bow for thousands of years.

When you rub two objects quickly together, you produce heat. This is how the friction bow works. First, find or cut a long, flat piece of softwood. Now cut a V-shaped notch into one end with a small, circular indentation at the point of the V. This piece of wood is called the "hearth." Next you need a strong, straight hardwood stick about 2ft (60cm) long and 1in (2.5cm) thick, sharpened to a point at one end and with a notch cut around the circumference of the stick about one-third of the length down from the blunt end. We'll call this the drill. For the bow, use a flexible branch about 2ft (60cm) long, made into a bow shape by using a piece of string or a shoelace. Finally, find a small square piece of wood big enough to fit comfortably in one hand,

and with an indentation cut into its middle. This is the "socket." To get the fire going, raise up the notched end of the hearth slightly using a stick, and place a large bundle of tinder under it. Now twist the bowstring once around the notch of the drill, and place the point of the drill on the indentation of the hearth. Put the socket on top of the drill so the drill is now held securely by the two pieces of wood. Move the bow backward and forward to turn the drill quickly—the friction will build up heat in the notch of the hearth, and create small burning embers of wood that drop through the notch onto the tinder and start the fire. Remember to have kindling and fuel nearby to use once the fire starts.

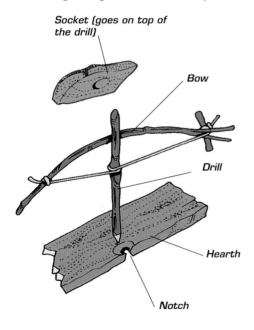

Socket (goes on top of the drill)

Bow

Drill

Hearth

Notch

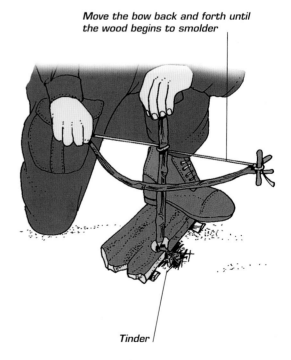

Move the bow back and forth until the wood begins to smolder

Tinder

TIP 26

Make Fire with a Flint

Hit some flint with a piece of metal and you get a shower of sparks. Now get some tinder and you have everything you need to make fire.

You can find natural flint in some areas, but the best tools for the job are professionally made flint and steel sets—buy these from any good camping or outdoor supplier. Most consist of a carbon-steel striker and a "flint," a striking surface specially made to produce lots of sparks. Some also include a magnesium block so you can shave off small pieces of highly flammable magnesium onto the tinder to make ignition easier. To start a fire using this method, first bundle up some tinder and get your kindling and fuel ready. Now place the flint at the bottom of the tinder, and strike it with the steel, moving the steel in the direction of the tinder. (Some sets have a steel saw that you draw across the flint.) This action should make a shower of sparks fall on the tinder and catch fire (it may take a few attempts). Blow on the tinder gently to encourage burning.

TRUE LIFE SURVIVAL !

It was the ability to make fire that helped save Jim and Suzanne Shemwell on a freezing mountain in Idaho. In March 2003, they set out on what should have been a three-hour snowmobile trip, but in a mountain valley they both became trapped in deep, powdery snow, and their snowmobiles stopped working. They didn't have much in the way of food or water, but they did have some cigarette lighters, a saw-and-shovel tool, and a rope. The weather became worse, and they realized that they weren't going to get rescued soon. So they made camp, digging out a snow cave. They also gathered firewood and made fires, taking turns watching over the fire to prevent it from going out. After a few days, once a horrible blizzard had passed, they set out to walk to rescue, making new camps and fires each night. After five days of surviving, they were eventually spotted by a rescue aircraft and were taken to safety.

Instant fire! Hold the flint very close to the bundle of tinder, and strike it in a downward direction with the steel. Make sure your tinder is bone dry in order for this fire-making method to work.

**TIP
27**

Make a Fire with a Magnifying Glass

When you are not using it to peer at bugs, a simple magnifying glass can help you start a roaring fire.

A small magnifying glass can be a lifesaver in the right circumstances, so carrying one into the wilderness is always a good idea. You can use it not only to study the local wildlife and to help you see when removing insect stingers, but also to start a fire on a sunny day. You first need to gather together all your fire-starting materials—tinder, kindling, and fuel. Choose a place for your fire and, in this case, make sure the location is in direct sunlight. (If this location is not good, you can always carry a smoldering stick or some embers wrapped in damp grasses and leaves to a new site, and use them to start a new fire there.) Hold the magnifying glass in one hand and angle it toward the sun. A circle of light will appear on the tinder, and you now move the magnifying glass slowly back or forward until this light is just a tiny, very bright point on the tinder. Hold it there, and after a few seconds the tinder should begin to smolder. Blow gently to turn the smoldering into flame.

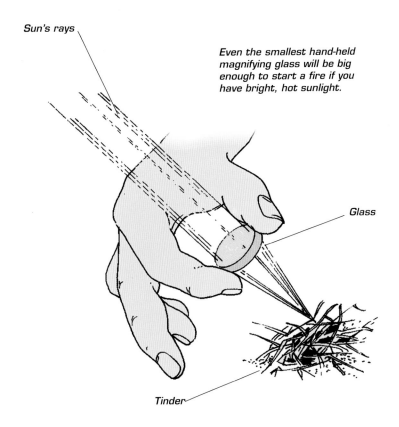

Sun's rays

Even the smallest hand-held magnifying glass will be big enough to start a fire if you have bright, hot sunlight.

Glass

Tinder

Make a Fire Plow

Don't ever be cold in the wild! You can start a fire just from a few pieces of wood and a handful of dry grass.

The fire plow has been used for fire-starting for thousands of years. It's similar to the bow and drill, but this time the hearth should have a long groove carved into it along its length. Cut a stick as before, but instead of using it as a "drill" you are going to use it as a "plow." Flatten off one end of the plow and make sure the stick is about the same width as the groove in the hearth. (As with the friction bow, the hearth should be made of softwood and the drill/plow of hardwood.) The fire plow works on a very simple principal. You place a bundle of tinder at one end of the hearth, and you sit at the other end. Slot the tip of the plow into the groove and start to rub it fast backward and forward. You may have to do this for some time—don't be surprised if you get out of breath—but eventually the heat builds up and tiny strips of smoldering wood are created in the groove. Push these onto the tinder at the end of the groove to start the fire going.

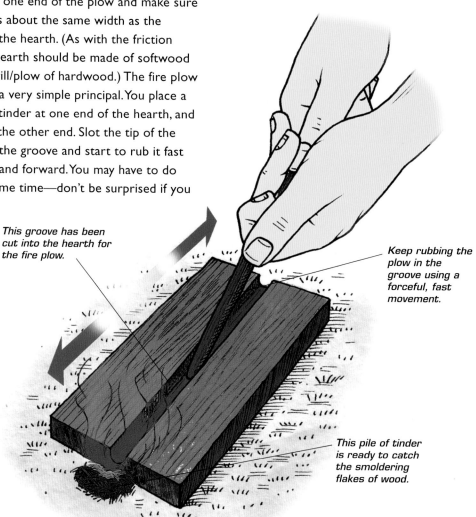

This groove has been cut into the hearth for the fire plow.

Keep rubbing the plow in the groove using a forceful, fast movement.

This pile of tinder is ready to catch the smoldering flakes of wood.

Make an Improvised Knife

Whether chopping up wood, skinning a rabbit, or even defending yourself against animal attack, a good knife is the tool to use.

A knife is essential for survival. It can be used for lots of tasks from cutting firewood through to preparing food, but when survival emergencies strike few people are usually carrying them. In that case, you can make a basic survival knive from natural materials and a few other odds and ends. It won't be as good as a professional knife, but it can help you with basic tasks. Be warned: improvised knives can be dangerous if not made properly. Always make sure that you cut away from yourself when using them. A basic but surprisingly sharp improvised knife can be made by trapping a piece of glass or metal (the lid off of a tin can is good) between a short, split branch. The split should run down only about half of the length of the wood, and can be made by carefully hammering in a sharp, wide stone from one end. Once the "blade" is inserted, tie lots of cord very tightly around the wood to hold the blade in place. Another type of blade can be made from stone or slate. Some naturally occurring stones are already very sharp, but you can "sharpen" a stone by chipping away at the edge with another stone, knocking off flakes to make an edge. Make sure you keep the flakes— they can make good arrow heads.

Safety first! Remember that improvised knives are nowhere near as strong as professionally made knives. Use them very carefully, and don't apply too much pressure to them at first.

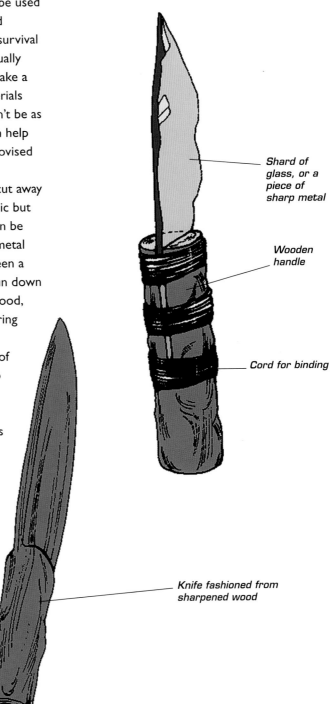

Shard of glass, or a piece of sharp metal

Wooden handle

Cord for binding

Knife fashioned from sharpened wood

TIP 30 Make a Bone Saw

To survive in the wild, you have to use your imagination. A piece of bone, for example, can even become a useful saw.

Saws are useful survival tools for cutting up wood and bone—you should include a professional wire saw in your survival tin or pack. If you haven't got a professional saw, however, you could try making a survival saw out of bone. Animal bones are usually easy to find if you keep your eyes open for them. The best bones for saws are large shoulder blades from big animals such as deer, bear, moose, or cattle. Check the bone over carefully for any cracks—if you find any don't use the bone because it won't be strong enough to make the saw. Now split the bone in half by striking it with a large, heavy stone. You can then make a sharp edge along where the bone split, which will be thinner and sharper already than the rest of the bone. Cutting "teeth" into the edge of the split using your knife will make a fairly sharp saw, one that is particularly good for cutting meat. Make sure you cut the teeth at regular intervals and don't make them too big, or it will be hard to saw through anything.

TRUE LIFE SURVIVAL

The Masai tribespeople of East Africa are the ultimate survivors. In a world of baking hot sunshine, little water, and dangerous animals, they still manage to live and thrive using survival skills that stretch back thousands of years. When a Masai warrior goes out on a hunting trip, for example, he travels very light so he doesn't exhaust himself in the African heat. He will usually only carry a hunting spear and a machete for cutting through undergrowth (and for preparing food). For food, however, he often uses a cunning survival technique. He cuts out the stomach lining of a goat, and then fills the lining with meat and fat. Then he twists up the "bag" and fastens it with home-made wooden pegs. The food is now protected in its own air-tight container.

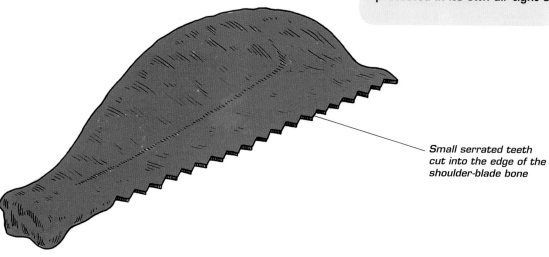

Small serrated teeth cut into the edge of the shoulder-blade bone

TIP 31

Make Camp Tools

To be good at survival, treat nature as your friend, not your enemy. See what you can make just by using wood, mud, bone, and grasses.

All it takes is a little of skill with a knife and an inventive mind to make some really useful camp tools and implements. Animal bones, for example, have been used as tools for centuries. Ribs can make needles, leg bones of large animals can be sharpened into spears or digging tools, and sharp teeth can be fixed to pieces of wood and used as cutting tools. For cooking, or for drying clothes near a fire, a pot stand is a useful thing to make. Cut or find two branches with forks at one end. Push the non-forked end of one stick upright into the ground so it is secure. Then take the other stick and push its forks into the ground a short distance from the other stick and weigh it down with rocks. Now

rest it on the forks of the other stick, and you can hang pans, food (for drying), and clothes from this device. You can try making storage pots out of natural clay. If you find clay-rich soil, break up the clay into small pieces, allow it to dry, then pick out impurities like stones. Wet the clay with water, and knead it until it can be shaped into a pot without cracking. You can then dry these near or even in a fire to make a basic storage jar. (Add sand or ground-up sandstone to the clay to stop it from cracking if you are going to harden the jar in a fire.)

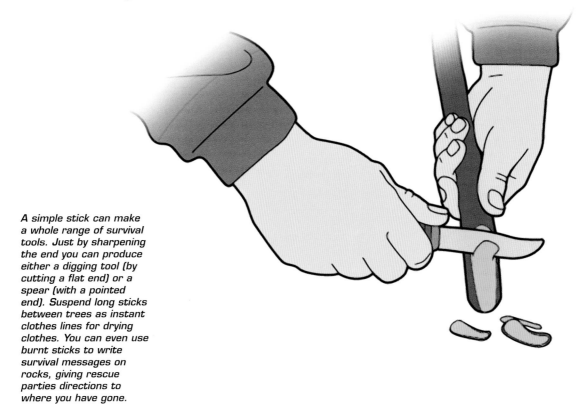

A simple stick can make a whole range of survival tools. Just by sharpening the end you can produce either a digging tool (by cutting a flat end) or a spear (with a pointed end). Suspend long sticks between trees as instant clothes lines for drying clothes. You can even use burnt sticks to write survival messages on rocks, giving rescue parties directions to where you have gone.

TIP 32

Make a Bark Container

You've gathered lots of berries and nuts to eat, so what do you put them in? Test your survival skills by making this practical bark container.

Cut a square section of birch bark (A) and soak the corners in water to make them flexible. Once you have done this, fold up the edge of the bark to a height of about 2–3in (5–8cm). Fold the corners inward and glue them into place by using tree resin (B)—look at the trunks of pine or birch trees to find this sticky material. You can also use this resin to paint over the finished product to make it waterproof (C). As the corners are drying, hold them in place by using short sticks partly split lengthways down the middle to act like clothes pegs (D). Remove the pegs once the container has dried. With practice and imagination, you'll be able to make different shapes of containers from bark. For practice, try to use bark from fallen trees, however, because cutting the bark from live trees can damage them.

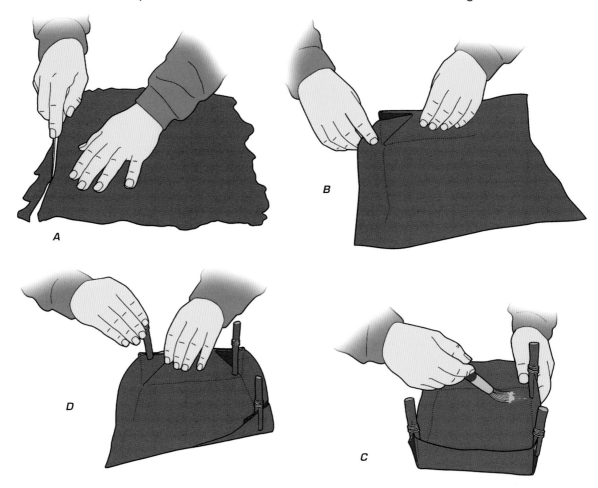

A

B

D

C

TIP 33 Make Rope

In survival speak, we make "cordage," not rope. Whatever it's called, it is vital for everything from binding shelters together to making bows.

A basic cordage is made from braiding strong, flexible plant stems or grasses together, though this cordage isn't the strongest. Bark is also an excellent source of cordage, particularly from trees such as the willow and lime. Cut out a long strip of bark (A), then cut this bark sheet down into thin strips (B). Allow them to dry out naturally. When you need to use them, soak them in water to make them flexible (C), then braid them into rope (D). A similar method of making cordage is possible with animal tendons. (The tendons are the strong pieces of tissue that connect muscles to bones.) If an animal has recently been killed, the tendons in the legs can be cut out and dried. Next, crush the dry tendons with stones until the fibers appear, then wet these to braid into shape. Animal skin itself is also suitable to drying and then cutting into strips to make into cordage. Most importantly, don't attempt climbing with whatever cordage you make—it won't be as strong as professional ropes.

TRUE LIFE SURVIVAL

If you find yourself in a survival situation, think clearly about what materials you have and how you can turn them into survival tools. One person who did just that was Poon Lim, a Chinese man who was stranded at sea for 130 days during World War II after his ship was sunk by a German submarine in the Atlantic Ocean. The raft was open and had little survival equipment, but Poon was a clever man. He took out a spring from inside his flashlight and used that to make fishing hooks. He also made some hooks out of nails that he pulled from the boat using his teeth. Unraveled rope served for fishing line, and whenever he caught a fish he cut it up using a "knife" made from the lid of a tin can. He also caught rainwater in his lifejacket. Though he came close to starvation, Poon was eventually picked up by another ship.

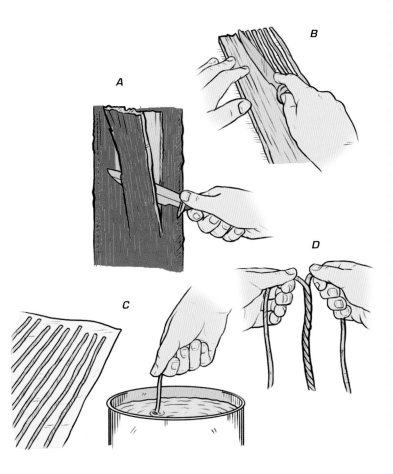

TIP 34 · Tie Knots

You might not think that being able to tie knots is important to survival. You'll change your mind if you try to build a raft or shelter.

I'll bet you can already tie a basic knot, but this is not necessarily a useful survival knot. The best kinds of knots are ones that are easy to tie but are also very secure. Not only that, but they should be easy to untie quickly when necessary. One of the most important functions of knots is for tying two ropes together. This is important for survival purposes because if you have made your own cordage the lengths are usually quite short. Two basic knots are shown here. First is the reef knot, which is used for binding two ropes together for light use—don't use this knot for heavy work. A more solid variation on this is known as the single sheet bend, which is also shown here. Practice simple knots like this over and over again until they become second nature. That way you'll be able to use them in the dark with confidence.

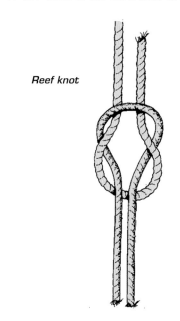

Reef knot

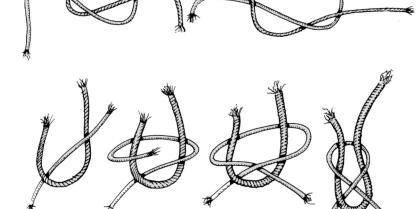

Tying a reef knot

Tying a single sheet bend

TIP 35 Tie Lashings

You are sailing a raft on white water when suddenly it starts to fall apart. The problem could be that you didn't use proper lashings...

While knots are useful, you also need to understand about lashings to make full use of ropes. Lashings are ways of tying two or more objects together, particularly objects like poles. Lashings are essential for making good shelters, platforms, and rafts, all of which need to be solidly tied together if they are to survive the elements. In these pictures, we see how to do two types of lashing—one to tie two parallel poles together, and the other to tie two cross members together. Think about how we could

use these lashings in shelters. The first lashing could be used when making a platform bed, tying the branches together securely. The second lashing would be good for tying on cross supports in an A-frame or lean-to shelter. Whenever you are using ropes or knots, always check that your rope is in good condition before use, and don't let the rope rub against anything with sharp edges. And when you aren't using a rope, make sure that you look after it—keep it dry and loosely coiled up.

TIP 36 Make Cooking and Eating Utensils

Just because you are in the wild and trying to survive doesn't mean that you have to eat like an animal.

A few simple cooking utensils will make a camp feel more like home and improve hygiene. For example, small branches can be turned into forks and spoons if you shape them a little by using a knife. When you are carving these, shape them in the same direction as the grain of the wood—this will make the tools stronger and more waterproof. Good woods for carving include sycamore, ash, and yew. To make a spoon, cut out a section of branch that has another branch coming off of it. The offshoot branch can be carved to form the handle of the spoon, while the bowl of the spoon is made naturally from the thick part of the main branch. You can also make a cup from a burl on a tree. This is a large, knobbly growth on the trunk, and simply by cutting it off and hollowing it out you have a cup. Two Y-shaped sticks stuck either side of a fire can hold a long stick over the fire, which in turn can be used for spit-roasting meats.

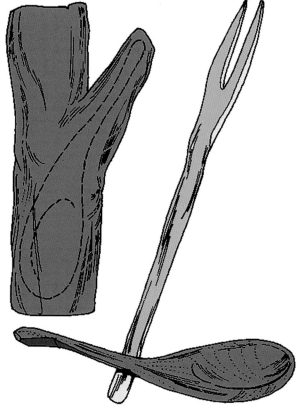

The spoon and fork above were both carved straight from a piece of tree wood. You can see how the natural shape of the wood was used to help form the spoon.

Simply take an old tin can, carefully punch three holes in the rim, and thread them with string. You now have a basic boiling pot, which you can hang by the string over a fire.

Tie a metal cooking pot to a forked twig to make an easy frying pan for cooking pieces of meat and fish. Make sure the forked twig is "green" and wet so it won't ignite while being held over the flame.

TIP 37 Make a Throwing Spear

Spears are one of history's ancient weapons. With a spear and a powerful throw—you can kill anything from fish to deer.

There are basically two types—a stabbing spear and a throwing spear, and the major difference between the two is length. The stabbing spear should be about 6ft (1.8m) long, while the throwing spear should be about 3ft (0.9m) long. The throwing spear will also have flights on the end to make it fly true. To make a basic spear, cut a long, straight branch to length and then form the point. The simplest way to make a point is simply to sharpen the wood with a knife and then harden the point over a fire. You can also make more advanced points by tying sharpened pieces of bone, metal, or glass to the end. For a throwing spear, cut a cross-shaped split in the blunt end of the wood and insert feathers or leaves to make flights. Throwing a

spear requires practice to master. Keep your eye on the target at all times and put your whole body weight into the throw. You can also increase the power by making a throwing device like the one shown.

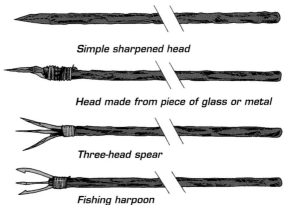

Simple sharpened head

Head made from piece of glass or metal

Three-head spear

Fishing harpoon

Spear thrower

A spear thrower is one way to get more power and distance when launching a spear. Sit the spear in the thrower, then put all your body weight into the throw. With practice you'll be able to shoot spears to distances of over 164ft (50m).

TIP 38

Make a Bow and Arrow

A deer pauses in a forest clearing—it thinks it's heard something. Now is the time for you to strike with your bow and arrow.

Bows can be difficult weapons to make, but even a simple one can bring you big success on a hunting trip. Shape the bow from a long branch of flexible hardwood—yew wood is the best. Cut a branch about 4ft (1.2m) long and carve it with your knife into a recognizable bow shape. Ensure that it is the same dimensions top and bottom, and that it widens slightly in the middle so you can hold it comfortably. Now cut notches about a half inch (1.25cm) from the end of each tip and tie strong cord between these two notches, bending the bow before tying to get a fast, springy feel. Arrows are made from straight sticks cut to about 2ft (60cm) long and just a quarter inch (6mm) in diameter, shaved of all bumps and protrusions. Make arrowheads/points in the same way that you would make a spear point (see Make a Throwing Spear, Tip 37), and put two or three flights into the other end, tying the flights on firmly. Also, cut a notch in the blunt end for the bowstring to sit in. Your bow is now ready to use. Practice against close targets, and gradually increase the distance. Focus on the target, not the arrow, and release the string smoothly when you fire (pull the string back with your index finger above the arrow and the next two fingers below).

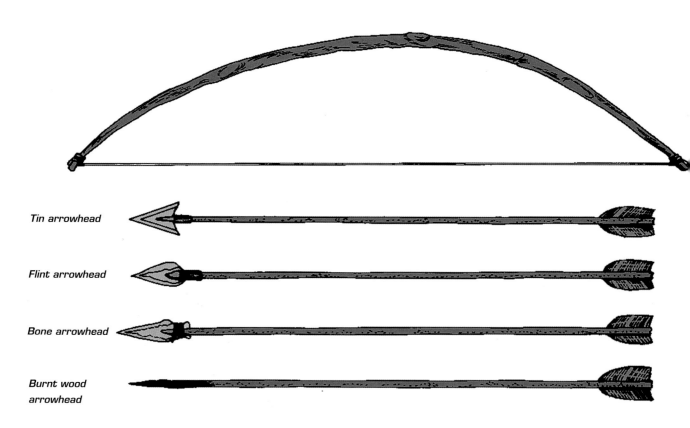

Tin arrowhead

Flint arrowhead

Bone arrowhead

Burnt wood arrowhead

Choose a strong but flexible piece of wood about 4ft (1.2m) long. Don't be afraid to make it shorter, however, if you find a long bow difficult to handle.

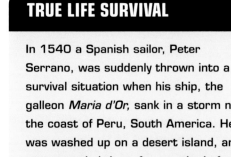

TRUE LIFE SURVIVAL !

In 1540 a Spanish sailor, Peter Serrano, was suddenly thrown into a survival situation when his ship, the galleon *Maria d'Or,* sank in a storm near the coast of Peru, South America. He was washed up on a desert island, and was stranded there for months before his rescue. One of the big problems he faced was getting enough to eat. Rather than hunting fast-moving animals, however, he killed turtles along the shoreline. Turtle meat helped him to stay alive, and turtle blood is also drinkable when it is fresh. A single turtle can provide up to four cups of blood, and this can be vital for survival if there is little drinkable water available. After the terrible Asian tsunami in 2004, some tribes surviving on remote islands cut off from help survived on almost nothing but turtles and the occasional wild boar.

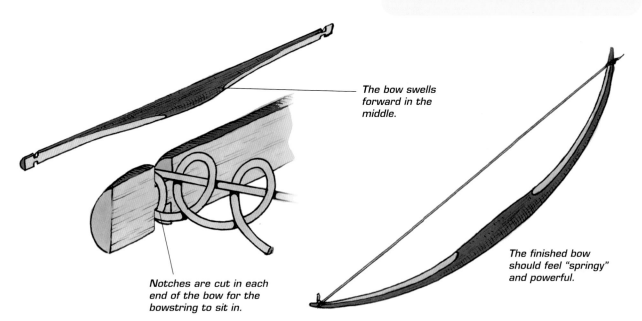

The bow swells forward in the middle.

Notches are cut in each end of the bow for the bowstring to sit in.

The finished bow should feel "springy" and powerful.

TIP
39 Make a Sling

A sling is a simple device with lots of power—remember that in the Bible's story of David and Goliath, David killed the towering Goliath using only a slingshot.

To make the slingshot, you need a piece of cord, or preferably a thick, heavy leather strip, that measures about 4ft (1.37m) or even longer. You also need a wider fabric pouch that slips onto the strap and can slide to the center (see picture). This is essentially all that you need to make a slingshot. To fire it, select a smooth stone that fits comfortably in the pouch. Now hold both of the loose ends in one hand (your throwing hand) and start to spin the slingshot around and around over your head, making sure the stone stays firmly in the pouch. Look at the target closely, and when the sling is whirring around very fast release one of the ends of the sling as the sling whips toward the target. The stone should go flying out at high speed. Slingshots take a lot of practice to master, so until you are used to them make sure that everyone stands a long way away from you in all directions.

The strip or cord needs to be very strong with no tears anywhere along its length. You don't want it snapping when it's whizzing above your head.

Make sure that the pouch fits right in the middle of the strip, otherwise it won't be an accurate weapon.

TIP 40 — Make a Catapult

Catapults are fun to use, but when you are hungry and need to catch food they can also be a serious hunting weapon.

Catapults are much easier to shoot accurately than slings, and most boys have experience of using them. The hard part about using them for survival is finding the materials to make one. The basic frame of the catapult is a Y-shaped piece of wood, cut from the fork of a tree branch. Try to cut a piece that has the fork at the top evenly spaced in relation to the handle below, and make sure the handle is long enough and wide enough to hold comfortably. You now need a piece of strong elasticized material. The best material to use is rubber surgical tubing (you should be able to get this from a big home repair store) or even the rubber from tire inner tubes. Clothing elastic is an easy option, but it is not as strong, so get the toughest brand you can. Make a pouch on the elastic in the center and tie the two ends around notches carved around the tops of the Y. To fire accurately, hold the catapult on its side and use the uppermost post of the Y as a type of sight.

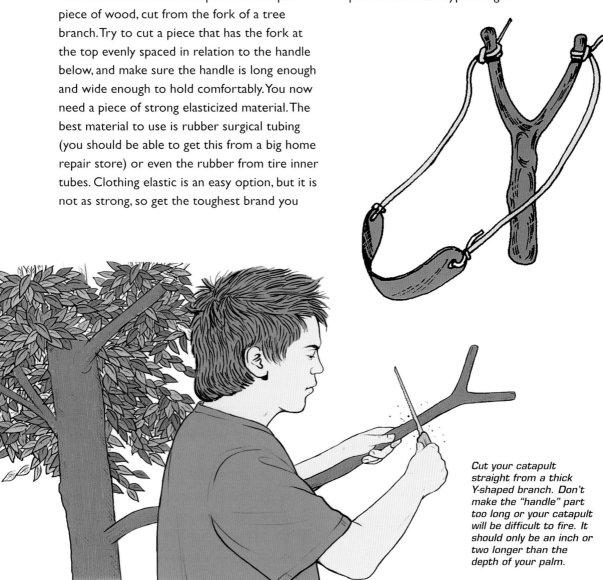

Cut your catapult straight from a thick Y-shaped branch. Don't make the "handle" part too long or your catapult will be difficult to fire. It should only be an inch or two longer than the depth of your palm.

TIP 41 Make a Bola

Take on running animals and even flying birds with the Bola, one of history's most ancient hunting weapons.

Bolas are lethally dangerous, so use one only with adult supervision. The basic materials for the Bola are five or six pieces of string, each about 3ft (1m) long. Tie them all together very tightly at one end. Now you need the same number of small weights—smooth rocks about the size of your palm will do. Wrap the stones in small pouches of material and then tie each string very tightly to each pouch. If you haven't got the material to make the pouches, simply tie the rope directly to the stone, wrapping it around several times to make it secure. You have now finished your Bola. To use it, hold it by the knotted ends and swing it fast above your head. Then release it at the target. It will spread out in the air as it flies, and if it hits the target the weights will kill or stun it, while the ropes will tangle the legs to bring it down.

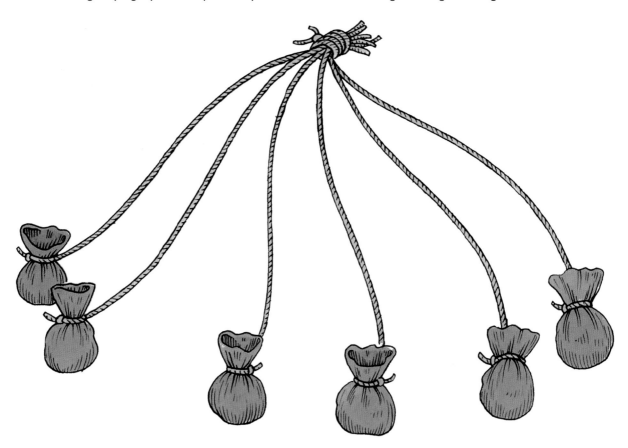

TIP 42

Make a Fishing Harpoon

A fish swims slowly in the summer current, unaware that you are waiting for it on the bank, armed with this fishing harpoon.

With some practice, harpooning is actually a great way of catching large fish fast. As with any hunting spear, the first thing you need is a long, straight branch, smoothed out with your knife. The spear should be longer than you are tall. The head of the spear is particularly important. Instead of carving the stick to a single point, you need to make multiple thin points—these will hold onto a slippery, wriggling fish better than one point. Make the head out of several long, sharp thorns or carve needles of sharp wood, and cut out notches in the spear end for these to sit in (A). Tie the spikes firmly in place (B), and it is a good idea to push a small piece of wood down between the thorns to make them splay out, improving your chances of a hit. When using the harpoon, stand completely still in fairly shallow, clear water, with your shadow falling onto the bank, not the water. Watch for a fish swimming nearby, and when it is in range thrust the spear straight into the water and into the fish. Immediately flip the fish out of the water onto the bank. Dinner's ready!

TRUE LIFE SURVIVAL

It's amazing what you can eat if you find yourself in a survival situation. Consider the story of Ricky Megee, who became lost in the Australian outback for 10 weeks in 2006 after his car broke down. The outback is a harsh place for survival—it seems barren, and it is full of dangerous creatures. Food is scarce, but Megee found just enough to eat from unexpected places. He ate raw leeches, which he simply plucked out of pools of water. Grasshoppers were also on the menu, which he ate raw. It was only frogs that he couldn't eat raw, fresh from the water. Instead, he spiked them on pieces of wire and let them dry out in the sun before eating. Although he was described as a "living skeleton" when he finally made it to safety, he had done enough to stay alive.

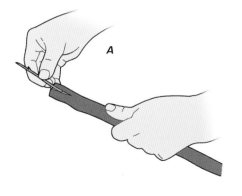

A

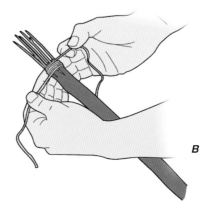

B

TIP 43 Track Wild Animals

A broken twig and a small footprint give you all the information you need. Your prey just walked this way.

Tracking wild animals needs all your senses and attention. The first step is to identify signs of an animal's presence. One of the best signs is a footprint in mud, dust, or soft earth—there are some pictures of common animal tracks opposite. But footprints aren't the only clues that an animal is nearby. Also look for droppings on the ground, particularly fresh ones (feces become crumbly the older they are), and any vegetation that has been damaged by an animal either pushing through it or eating it. Squirrels, for example, will often strip the bark from tree branches, and some animals will scratch tree

trunks. There may also be pieces of fur caught on sharp branches, and piles of bones or nut shells may indicate that an animal has been feeding recently. Better still, you may also find an animal den with fresh earth and other debris piled outside—combined with some fresh droppings and footprints, this means that an animal could be home. Once you have found a piece of "sign," try to find another one or two pieces nearby. When you have three pieces of sign, you can usually get a good idea of the direction the animal was headed, particularly if the sign is along a well used track.

Walking animals often leave diagonal tracks like these.

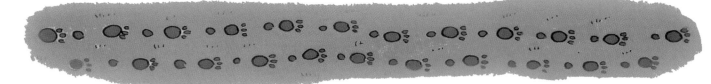

The tracks of smaller animals tend to bunch up more closely to one another.

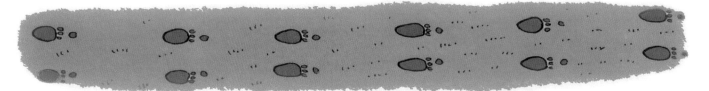

When an animal is running the distance between the tracks opens up.

TIP 44 Identify Animal Footprints

You've discovered some animal tracks. Now you need to work out what animal it is and where it's going.

Identifying an animal from its tracks is not easy, especially because tracks become more worn over time. A general rule is that the sharper the print, the more recently it was made. Old prints become crumbly around the edges and filled with leaves, twigs, and dirt. Whenever you are attempting to identify a track, pay attention to the following features:

1) the number of pads or toes, and the number of nails or claws—but remember that some animals don't use their nails or claws when they are walking;

2) the overall size of the track, and the distance between each print—generally, the longer the step, the bigger the animal;

3) the type of pattern the tracks make on the ground—the tracks will become more spaced out as an animal runs.

Trace the shape of the track with the tip of your finger, because this will make the outline clearer in your mind's eye. Once you have as much information as possible, compare it against the footprint pictures here, or against those in another field guide.

Grizzly bear

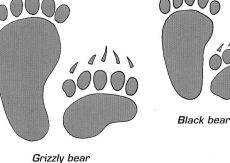

Black bear

Otter

Dog

Wolf

Cougar

Squirrel

Hare

Deer

Moose

Goose

Duck

TIP 45

Stalk Wild Animals

When hunting a super-sensitive wild animal, you need all your cunning and patience to get into hunting range.

Stalking is not easy—animals' senses are much better than ours, and creatures are spooked by the tiniest movements and sounds. The first principle of stalking is to keep downwind of the animal. This means that the wind is carrying your smell away from the animal, not toward it. An animal such as a deer will be able to smell you from hundreds of yards away. Move toward the animal very, very slowly, keeping yourself down behind cover such as bushes, shrubs, trees, and high pieces of ground and crawling if necessary. Watch that you don't step or kneel on twigs or other objects that might crack and alert the animal. If the animal suddenly appears to sense that you are there and goes still, freeze immediately in whatever position you are in. Animal eyesight usually works by detecting movement rather than color, so stay completely still until the animal goes back to feeding or whatever it was doing. The aim is to get so close to the animal that you are able to use your hunting weapons.

TRUE LIFE SURVIVAL !

The Nukak Indians live today in a very remote part of the Amazon rainforest in South America. They still use the traditional methods of hunting that have been passed down for thousands of years. One of their major foods is monkeys, which they hunt in the trees by using blowpipes. The blowpipes are made from hollowed-out pieces of wood or reeds, and they are many feet long. The darts fired out of the blowpipes are made from long thorns that are dipped in powerful natural poisons from plants and reptiles, poisons strong enough to kill a grown monkey. The Nukak hunters use sound as much as sight when they hunt—they listen for the noise of the monkeys rustling through the trees, and fire in the direction of the sound. The biggest threats to the Nukak come from modern peoples cutting down their forest for logs, and diseases from the outside world.

The flat crawl is a really stealthy but very slow way of moving.

The crawl is good for keeping hidden but moving steadily.

The stalking crouch allows you to move really quickly but it is easier for animals to see you.

TIP 46

The Deadfall Trap

Deadfall traps are dead simple. They work by dropping a heavy weight right onto the prey, killing it by the crushing force.

Making a deadfall trap can be as easy or as difficult as you want. The simplest of all deadfall traps involves putting a piece of food bait onto the ground, tying a heavy log or stone to a long piece of rope, throwing the rope over a tree branch, and then pulling the weight up into the air over the bait. Hidden from view and away from the trap, you hang onto the end of the rope until something crawls up to the bait, then you release the rope. However, such a trap means that you have to sit still for ages,

getting cold and bored. The deadfall trap shown here is one you can make and leave. Make the support and trigger mechanism first, then set up the deadfall logs on top of the support. Remember, never stand underneath a deadfall trap when you are making it, or you could become its first victim.

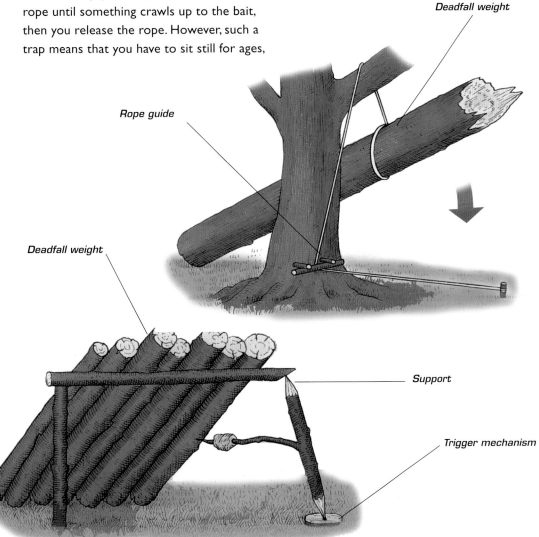

Deadfall weight

Rope guide

Deadfall weight

Support

Trigger mechanism

TIP 47

The Basket Trap

The basket trap takes a lot of effort to make, but it is a good way to catch lots of fish very quickly.

Basically, you have to weave together lots of thin, flexible branches into a basket shape that is wide at one end and narrow at the other. Make the branches very close together, and tie them in a grid pattern with cord. The entrance to the basket should narrow down into a funnel shape. Cover the whole basket with a thin net to stop any fishes that go into the trap from escaping. The way the basket trap works is that fish swim in through the narrow funnel opening and then get trapped inside the body of the basket, unable to escape the way they came. You should leave the basket facing into fast-flowing water at a narrow part of the river or stream. Positioning the basket in this way will mean that fish are swept into it, and you can even pile up stones around the trap so that the fish are forced to swim into it. If you do this, check it every few minutes to see if you have caught anything.

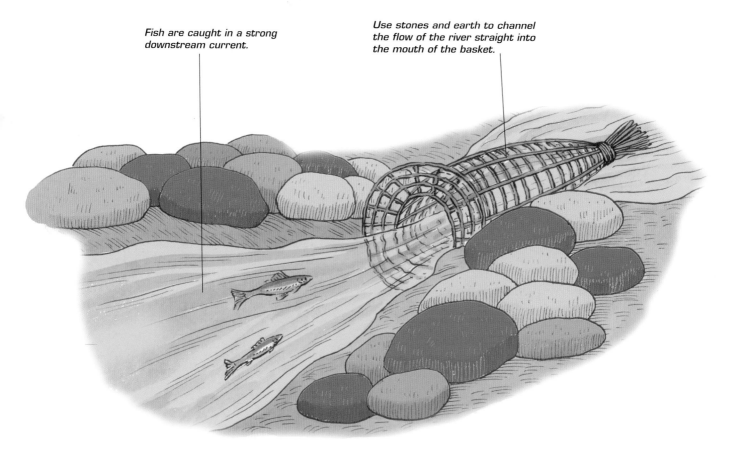

Fish are caught in a strong downstream current.

Use stones and earth to channel the flow of the river straight into the mouth of the basket.

TIP 48 Make a Snare

Don't have a bow or gun? You can go hunting with nothing more than just a coil of thin wire.

Snaring is illegal or strictly controlled in many countries. Make sure that an adult supervises you. Also, be careful if you make a trap in your own backyard—you don't want to injure or kill a family pet. A snare is a thin piece of wire that has a loop at one end—as shown below. Make sure the loop can close quickly and tightly if something pulls inside it. Depending on the law, you can also buy professional self-locking snares from some hunting and outdoor retailers. The important skill in using a snare is how you place it. Locate it near the mouth of an animal burrow or along a well used animal track. Raise the snare up a few inches from the ground using short sticks, and make sure that no vegetation will get caught when it works. Any animal that puts its head through the snare will be caught as the loop closes. Animals are not often killed by snares (they hold the animal for you to kill later), so it is important to check the trap regularly to prevent unnecessary suffering.

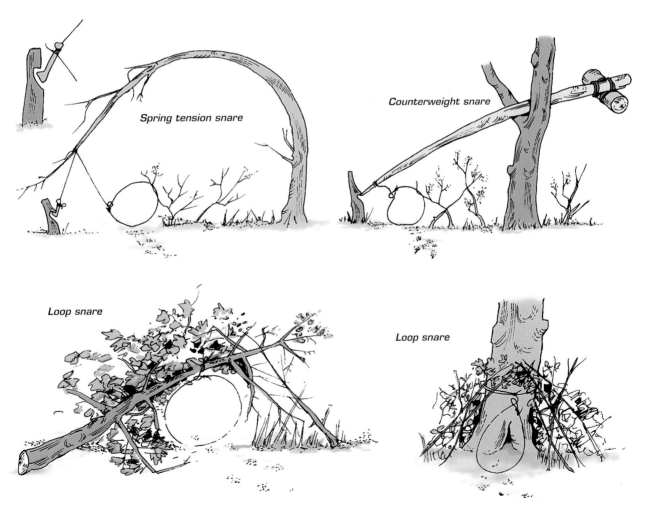

Spring tension snare

Counterweight snare

Loop snare

Loop snare

TIP 49

Prepare a Rabbit

You've killed your first rabbit, and need to get it ready to eat. Now comes the gruesome part.

Rabbits are found all around the world, so they make a good survival food. (However, you cannot survive on rabbits alone—the meat takes more nutrients to digest than it gives you, so if you ate nothing but rabbit you would be bringing your own death closer.) It's therefore important that you know how to prepare a rabbit for eating. First, squeeze its belly hard with your thumb, pressing downward. This shoots out any urine from the rabbit's bladder—you don't want to eat meat that tastes like urine! Now, lift up the belly skin and with a very sharp knife slit the skin from the chest to the anus (A). Ease the skin away from the stomach, and now cut very carefully through the stomach wall itself (B)—avoid cutting any internal organs. Once you have done this, scoop or shake out the rabbit's innards. Now slice through the rest of the skin, down the legs and up the skin, and then peel it off completely (C and D). Cut off the rabbit's head and wash the carcass, and it is now ready to cook.

TIP 50 Preparing Larger Animals

You've brought down a deer after an hour of hard hunting. With careful preparation, you now have enough food to feed you for week.

To skin a large animal, it is easier if you can string it up by the back legs from a tree, but this is not always possible. Skinning a deer works in a similar way to skinning a rabbit. First, bleed the animal by slashing its throat deeply and let the blood run out. Catch this blood. It is nutritious in its own right. Then cut carefully around the anus or penis (A) and insert two fingers to lift up the belly skin (B). Carefully cut through this skin up to the neck (C), making sure you don't cut the membrane around the stomach (D). Then roll the animal on its side and pull out the innards (E). Cut out and remove the anus, and saw off the head. Cut the legs off at the first joints, and now you can slowly pull all the skin off—keep this for making shelters and clothes. Finally, cut the carcass up into joints for cooking. Follow the natural lines of muscles to get the best cuts.

A

B

C

D

E

TIP 51 Make a Fishing Rod and Hooks

When hunger starts to bite, fishing could be your best way of surviving.

If you have a professional fishing rod with you, that's great, but you can make your own fishing rod if necessary. First you need a rod. This can be nothing more than a long branch. Just choose a young green one that is flexible but strong. If you have some fishing line, split weights, and hooks in your survival tin, all you need to do is tie a piece of line to the end of the rod, put on a hook and a weight (the weight keeps the hook under the water), find some bait for the hook (worms, insects, or maggots), and then you are ready to go fishing. If you don't have this equipment, use any sort of thin cordage for the line and sections cut from a thorny bush to make the hooks—the picture on this page will show you how to do this. Buttons or small stones can act as the weights, and pieces of cork or wood are great as floats. Finally, bright objects such as feathers are good as lures for fish. When you fish, try shaded places or, in cold climates, try sunny patches, and choose places where the water flows more slowly and where you can see bubbles and ripples from feeding fish.

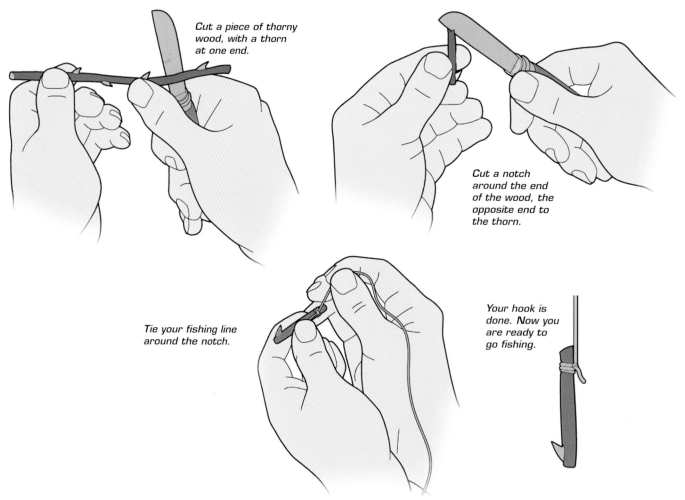

Cut a piece of thorny wood, with a thorn at one end.

Cut a notch around the end of the wood, the opposite end to the thorn.

Tie your fishing line around the notch.

Your hook is done. Now you are ready to go fishing.

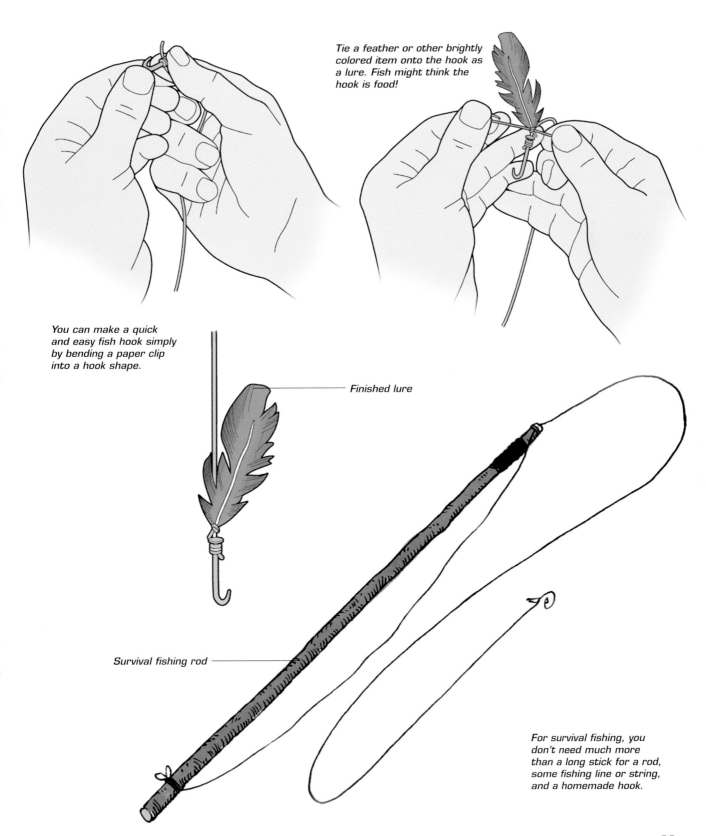

Tie a feather or other brightly colored item onto the hook as a lure. Fish might think the hook is food!

You can make a quick and easy fish hook simply by bending a paper clip into a hook shape.

Finished lure

Survival fishing rod

For survival fishing, you don't need much more than a long stick for a rod, some fishing line or string, and a homemade hook.

TIP 52 Make a Bottle Trap

How do you go fishing without a line or net? It is easy if you happen to have an empty plastic bottle.

The problem with the bottle trap is that it is good for trapping only relatively small fish, but in a survival situation they could be the difference between life and death. The bottle trap requires nothing more than a large plastic bottle. Using a sharp knife, cut off the top of the bottle about one-third of the bottle's length from the spout. Then turn the head of the bottle around and insert it back into the body (make sure that you have removed the cap). When the bottle is immersed in a river or stream, fish can swim through the neck into the body of the bottle, where they become stuck for you to collect later. Put some pieces of river vegetation in the back of the bottle—fish will be more interested in exploring this than an empty bottle. Once you've caught the fish, be careful. Don't open the bottle up over the river or you will risk losing the fish back into the water.

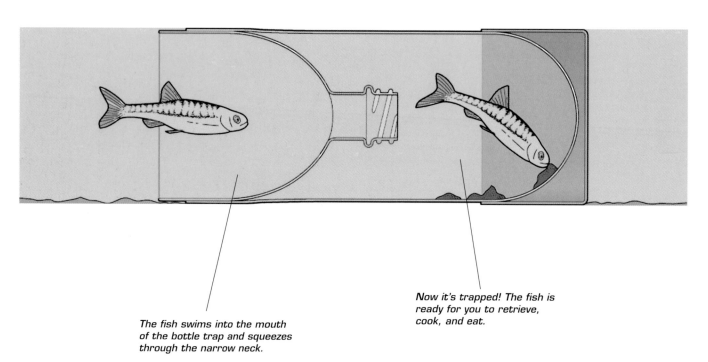

The fish swims into the mouth of the bottle trap and squeezes through the narrow neck.

Now it's trapped! The fish is ready for you to retrieve, cook, and eat.

TIP 53 Line Fishing

If you have a stream or river nearby, you don't have to go hungry in the wild. Here's a way to catch as many fish as you need.

One good way to raise your chances of a big catch is by using lots of lines suspended in the water overnight. To do this, first take a length of rope and tie several pieces of fishing line to it, each with its own hook, weights, and bait. Make the fishing lines of different lengths. This means you will be able to fish at different levels of the water, tempting different fish. (Or you can also attach floats at varying positions along the lines.) Now find a narrow stream and embed two short sticks into the banks across from each other. Tie the piece of rope between the two sticks so that the fishing lines dangle into the water. Leave this fishing line overnight in the water and get up bright and early to check if you have caught anything. If you leave it too long into the day, other animals may steal your catch.

Line fishing is a great way to hunt for food while you go away and do something else! You can attach as many lines as you want, but two or three will do a good job.

TIP 54 Preparing Fish

You've caught some fish. Now you are ready for one of the great survival meals. Simply prepare the fish using the steps below.

The easiest way to prepare a fish is to gut it. You need a very sharp knife for this, so be careful. Take the fish and slit along its belly from the neck to the tail (A). Now open up the fish and scoop out all of its innards (B). Wash out the body cavity, cut off the tail and the fins, and the fish is now ready to cook (C). Be careful when eating it that you don't swallow a bone.

Another way of preparing a fish is called filleting. In this case, cut open and gut the fish as described. Now cut off all the fins, the tail, and head (D). With these removed, you can sometimes simply pull the fish meat off the bones, leaving you with nice, boneless pieces that will cook quickly over the fire (E and F). Don't throw away the fish bones, however. Fish ribs are extremely sharp and can be used to make improvised needles. You may find, though, that you are wasting too much valuable meat by filleting. If so, go back to the first method for preparing the fish.

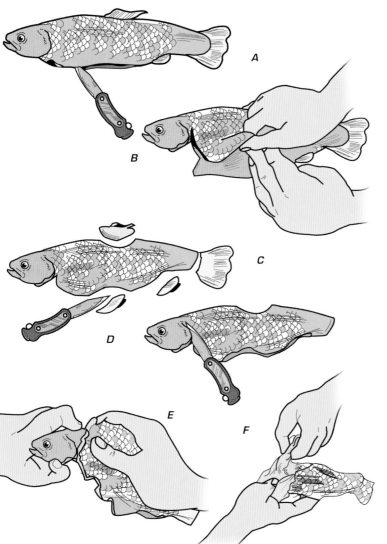

TRUE LIFE SURVIVAL !

In 2006 came reports of one of the greatest survival stories ever. Three Mexican fisherman had set sail from their Pacific port in October 2005, heading out in a 27-ft (8.2-m) boat. However, problems with their motors meant they were eventually swept right out into the ocean—they would eventually be taken by currents more than 5,000 miles (8,046km) from their starting point. They were lost at sea for nine months. During that time, their greatest problem was the lack of food and water. Using the nets and lines they had on board, they managed to catch just enough fish to stay alive, while rain provided some drinking water. The men were finally rescued by a Taiwanese tuna-fishing ship.

TIP 55

Make a Yukon Stove

If you can make a Yukon stove, you are truly becoming a survival expert. It's got everything you need for warmth and cooking.

A Yukon stove is an advanced survival fire, but it's one that's great for both cooking and heat. The first step is to dig a hole in the ground about 9in (24cm) across and 1ft (30cm) deep. Then dig a channel into the hole—you're going to use this to feed the fire with fuel and control its air flow. (Remember how important air is to fire.) Once you've done this, stack up rocks around the edge of the hole, creating a sort of chimney for the fire, and making sure you don't close off the channel at the bottom. Pack the

rocks with mud and clay to keep them stable. The heat of the fire will bake the clay to make the structure more solid. Your Yukon stove is now ready. Use the channel at the bottom to push fuel into the fire. Once lit, the Yukon stove produces a lot of heat, and you can control the blaze by using rocks or pieces of wood to alter the amount of air feeding the fire through the channel or the chimney. Food is baked either inside the oven, or can be cooked on wooden skewers or a wood "grill" over the chimney.

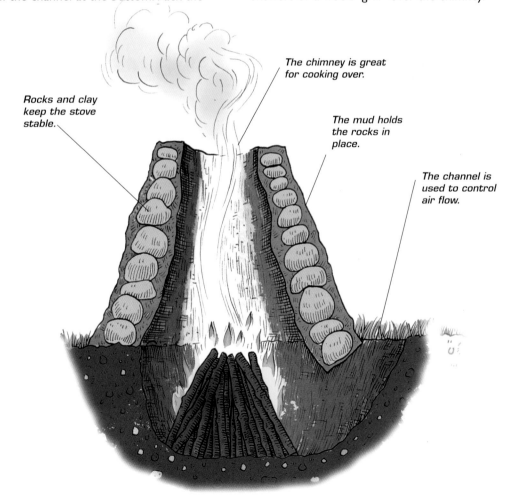

Rocks and clay keep the stove stable.

The chimney is great for cooking over.

The mud holds the rocks in place.

The channel is used to control air flow.

TIP 56 Make a Steam Pit

Burying your food in a steaming pit might not sound like a good way of cooking. Don't be fooled—here's how to cook perfect meals.

A steam pit is a superb method of cooking for survival because it keeps all the goodness in the food. Dig a short trench in the ground about 1ft (30cm) deep and build a fire in the bottom. Now make a grill of dry sticks over the trench, with rocks spread across the sticks (A). The rocks will become red hot and eventually fall through into the trench. Once the fire is starting to die down, brush away the burning embers with a bunch of sticks and push a long stick into the center of the trench. Now cover the rocks with a deep layer of thick, green grasses (B). Wrap your food tightly in more green leaves, place on the bed of grass, then cover the whole trench over with another layer of grass (C), then a layer of soil. Now pull out the protruding stick, pour a small amount of water into the hole, fill the hole with soil, and leave everything alone for 20 minutes or so (D). Inside the pit, the steaming rocks will perfectly cook your food. Dig it up carefully and unwrap it to eat.

TIP 57 Cook Over a Fire

A blazing campfire under the evening sky and a few cooking skills are all it takes to cook great dishes at the end of a day in the wild.

The simplest way to cook over a fire is simply to skewer meat or vegetables on sticks and suspend them over the flames like a barbecue. You can also make a grill lattice of sticks, placing this over the fire by using Y-shaped supports at each corner or piles of rocks. One important point is to make sure that meat is properly cooked through—fire can char meat on the outside but leave it uncooked on the inside. The best way to check whether meat is cooked is to push a skewer or sharp knife into a thick part of the meat near a bone. If the juices that run out are bloody, the meat is not cooked. If they run out clear, it is ready to eat. There are other ways to cook over a survival fire. You can bake small fish or thin strips of meat directly on hot, clean rocks that have been heated in the flames (see the pictures below). You can also wrap meat in plant materials, then cover the "parcel" in soil and make a fire over the top of it. The heat will bake the meat inside the parcel, while the soil protects it from getting charred.

A) Pile up some large, smooth rocks.

B) Make a fire on top of the rocks.

C) When the fire dies down, brush away the embers.

D) Lay the fish on the red-hot rocks to cook.

TIP 58

Dry Foods with Smoke and Air

In a survival situation, you don't have fridges and freezers to keep your food fresh. Act quickly, or all your food will rot.

The moisture in food quickly attracts mold and bacteria, so if you want to store food for any length of time you need to dry it out. If you are in a warm, dry climate, you can dry nonfatty meats (like fish and poultry) and vegetables in the air. Leave small pieces of the meat or vegetables on rocks or hung over branches in the warm air and sunshine, ideally with a warm breeze blowing over them until they are completely dried out. However, this can take some time, and you need to watch the food to make sure that it doesn't rot, get stolen by animals, or covered in insects. A quicker way of drying is smoking. Smoke draws out moisture from foods, and a simple way of smoking is to place food on a grid of twigs over a very smoky fire. You can make the fire smoky by adding lots of green leaves and grasses, almost smothering the fire. Don't let the fire show open flames because you don't want to cook the food. To eat dried food, you may have to soak it in water first to rehydrate it and make it ready for cooking.

Smoking food is the best way of drying it out quickly.

A drying frame uses air to dry your food, but watch out for animals trying to steal your dinner!

TRUE LIFE SURVIVAL !

In February 2007, two friends went missing in the jungles of French Guiana, a country on the northeastern coast of South America. They were Loic Pillois and Guilhem Nayral, both experienced outdoorsmen. Once they had been missing for a couple of weeks, a major search effort was launched because the two men had intended to go into the jungle for only 10 days. By the end of March, there was still no sign of them, and the search was scaled down. Then, seven weeks after they first went missing, the two men reappeared, dehydrated and exhausted but alive. They had survived by drinking river water and by eating insects, plant seeds, and two turtles that they managed to trap in a river. This simple diet had kept them alive.

TIP 59 Make Wild Teas

A pine tree doesn't look like a good survival food at first glance. Yet as well as providing pine nuts to eat, the pine tree gives you everything you need for a refreshing drink.

Boiling is another way of cooking survival foods, particularly tough vegetables and plant materials that need to be softened before you can eat them. Once you've finished cooking, however, don't just throw the water away. If you've been cooking vegetables, the water will contain some of the goodness from the food, so once it has cooled you can drink it. You can also make a simple tea in the wild using just two teaspoons of crushed pine needles and a cup of water. Boil the water first to make it safe to drink, then take it off the boil and add the pine needles. (When you pick the pine needles, choose the greenest, freshest ones because these will have a better taste than older needles.) Let the needles sit in the water for at least 10 minutes. Then strain the liquid into another container through a piece of fabric, removing the pine needles. You are left with a refreshing, nutritious drink.

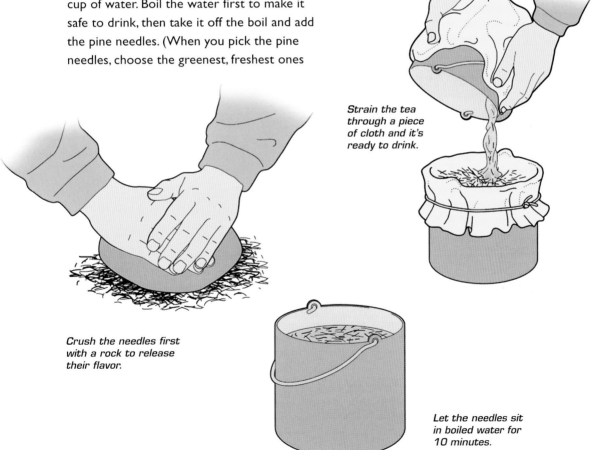

Strain the tea through a piece of cloth and it's ready to drink.

Crush the needles first with a rock to release their flavor.

Let the needles sit in boiled water for 10 minutes.

TIP 60

Easy and Safe Plant Foods

Nature is full of good things to eat, if only you know where to look…

Some highly poisonous plants look like edible ones, so you have to follow a good plant identification guide and ask a knowledgeable adult. Yet there are some very common plants that are easily accessible for survival. Stinging nettles are perfectly edible and contain vitamins, iron, and protein, but pick only the youngest leaves from the top of the plant (using gloves, of course). Boil the leaves in water—this kills off the stinging chemicals completely and makes the leaves safe to eat. During late summer, blackberries and raspberries are easily found in many natural areas, and after washing can be eaten straight from the bush. We have already seen how pine tree needles can be used to make a nutritious drink, but pine cones also contain delicious nut seeds, which you can eat raw or roasted. You can even eat acorns to survive, although they do taste horrible uncooked. Take the shell off and boil the acorns several times, changing the water each time. This helps to make them less bitter.

Pine kernel

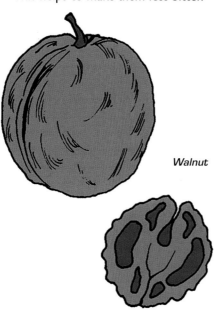

Walnut

Field mushroom

Acorn

Blackberries

Nettles

TIP 61 Spot Poisonous Plants

Some plants are great to eat, while others taste horrible. Some, however, are so lethal that they can kill you after a few mouthfuls.

Here are a few general rules about identifying plants that are dangerous. Don't eat any plants that have white or yellow berries, and avoid plants with red berries unless you are positive that they are OK (such as raspberries). Don't eat any plants that make your skin itch when you touch them, or that have small, barbed hairs on them. Never eat plants that smell of almonds when you crush up the leaves—these can contain a deadly poison. Obviously, don't consider plants as food if they are dead, rotting, or show signs of being infested with insects.

Never eat plant bulbs. Also, don't be fooled into thinking that a plant is safe to eat because you see animals eating it—some animals are able to eat substances that would make us very sick. You should also avoid fungi (mushrooms and toadstools). There are lots of edible ones out there, but there are also some varieties that are lethal. Until you are absolutely certain you know the difference it is best to play it safe.

Death cap mushroom

Giant puffball

Foxgloves

Water hemlock

Deadly nightshade

TIP 62 Insects as Food

Insects might sound like the worst thing in the world to eat, but in a survival situation they can be a life-saving food.

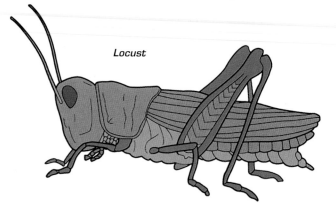

Locust

Worker termite

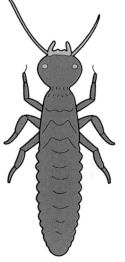

Termite without wings

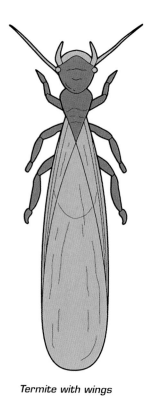

Termite with wings

Insects contain large amounts of protein for their size, and protein is essential for building up and repairing our muscles. Crickets, locusts, and grasshoppers can be eaten, but you should first pull off their wings, legs, and antennae. As horrible as it may seem, termites are also great survival food, and they provide lots of protein, fat, and water (a good combination in a survival situation). Boil all insects to make them safe to eat. You can also eat caterpillars in the same way, but avoid the hairy specimens, which may contain irritating chemicals. Special forces soldiers are often taught to eat earthworms as a survival food. Squeeze out the insides first, then either fry or boil them. If the thought of eating these is too much for you, dry them out in the sun or on a hot stone, then grind them up into a powder using a stone. You can add this powder to other dishes to give yourself an extra protein boost. Avoid eating any insects that are dead or diseased, very brightly colored, or which smell bad.

To collect termites, poke a stick into a termite mound. The termites will attack the stick, and grip on with their jaws.

Pull out the stick, then simply scrape the termites off the stick into a cooking pot

TRUE LIFE SURVIVAL !

Today we tend to think of insects as survival food only, but throughout history many peoples have classed insects as part of a normal, healthy diet. Roman and Greek citizens, for example, used to dine on beetle larvae and cicadas, and in the ancient Middle East locusts were often eaten with honey as a delicacy. Crickets were a major part of the diet of many Native American peoples during the nineteenth century. And insects continue to be eaten to this day. Throughout many parts of Africa, Asia, and Latin America, people still consume large amounts of insect food, ranging from termites to spiders. In fact, in some remote jungle parts of Asia and Latin America, the people even eat tarantula spiders. Though insects might seem disgusting to eat, they are actually one of our oldest foods.

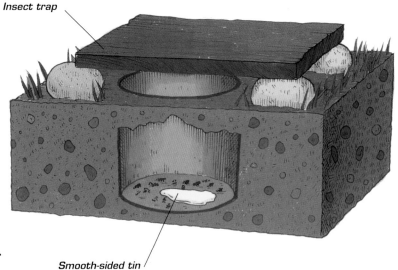

Insect trap

Smooth-sided tin

An insect trap is made by burying a smooth-sided pot up to its rim in the ground with some water in the bottom. Make some shade over it with a board. The insects crawl under the board in search of shelter and moisture and fall into the pot.

TIP 63

Survive a Snake Attack

You step over a fallen log without thinking, and suddenly see a snake, coiled up ready to strike. What do you do?

The first rule of encountering a snake in the wild is to give it as much space as possible. Snakes will not attack humans unless they are provoked, usually by a person accidentally stepping on them. Be on the lookout for snakes when walking through the wilderness, and be extra careful when exploring under rocks or in shady areas in hot countries. Snakes like to get out of the sun as much as you do. If you see a snake, simply walk in the opposite direction without hurrying, and everything should be fine. In some situations, however, a snake may attack with lightning speed. If you have the chance, hit the snake on the head with a club or even cut it off with a machete. Be careful if the snake appears to be dead—sometimes snakes play dead, then attack when you try to pick them up. If the worst happens and you are bitten, look at the bite marks. If there are two large puncture holes separate from other teeth, then the snake is probably poisonous and you need to get to medical help fast. If possible, send someone else to get help while you stay as calm as possible—the faster your heart beats, the quicker the poison will pump around your body.

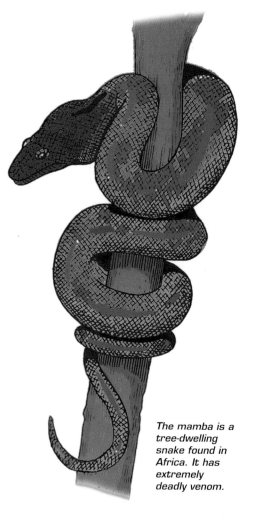

The mamba is a tree-dwelling snake found in Africa. It has extremely deadly venom.

The boomslang is a venomous snake found in desert regions.

TIP 64

Survive a Bear Attack

Of all the powerful creatures you don't want to meet in the wild, a bear must be one of the worst.

Bears will attack only if they feel they or their cubs are threatened. If you are walking through dense forest in an area where you know there are bears, call out every few minutes. This action alerts the bear that you are coming, and gives it a chance to move away. If you suddenly come face to face with a bear, start talking to it softly and raise your hands straight above your head to make yourself look as big as possible. Don't be tempted to run—this will make the bear chase you, and it can run much faster than you can. Instead, back away slowly. If a bear does start to push you around, curl up in a ball on the ground and try not to respond to pushes, scratches, and bites. By playing dead, you may convince the bear that you are not a threat and he will leave you alone. If the attack is life-threatening, however, fight back with as much noise as you can, using sticks to jab at the bear and, hopefully, drive it away.

TRUE LIFE SURVIVAL !

Deep in the heart of the country in Montana in 1823, the trapper and frontiersman Hugh Glass suffered a horrific attack after he surprised a grizzly bear and her cubs. He was terribly injured, even though his companions managed to shoot and killed the bear. Some men stayed with the injured Glass, but they feared attacks by local Native peoples and eventually abandoned him there in the wilderness. Yet Glass was tough, and he knew how to live off of the land. He began an epic 100-mile (160-km) crawl through the wilderness, living off wild fruit and dead animals he found along the way. Rivers and rainwater provided him with fluids. Despite all the dangers he faced, Glass survived and reached safety six months later.

Bear paw prints

TIP 65
Survive a Cougar Attack

Cougars or mountain lions will rarely attack humans unless they are threatened, but old or injured lions have sometimes killed people as a source of easy prey.

Preventing a cougar attack is easier than surviving one. In areas where cougars live, don't walk alone and be extra careful at dawn and dusk because this is when cougars often hunt. Make lots of noise as you move to alert the cougar to your presence. If you have a dog with you, keep it on a leash because if it strays, the cougar will see it as an animal separated from its pack. (It is actually best not to take your dog with you—cougars will regard it as prey.) If you do see a cougar, don't approach it. Stay still and let it move away from you. If it does approach, look it in the eye, stand up straight, and raise your arms and jacket high above your head, to make yourself look big and powerful. If it

attacks, fight as hard as you can using rocks, sticks, noise, and anything else you can think of. Remember—the cougar will want an easy kill, so make sure that you don't give in.

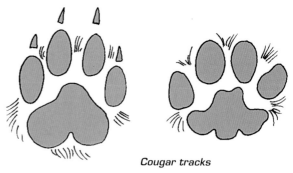

Cougar tracks

TIP 66

Survive Falling into a River

Falling into a river is not like falling into a swimming pool. Strong currents and underwater obstacles can drag you under in seconds.

There are many dangers in a river, including strong currents and dangerous underwater objects, such as rocks. If the river is flowing slowly, and you can swim straight to the side safely, then obviously you should do so. However, if the river is flowing fast you may have more problems. First, don't try to swim directly into the current—it will be stronger than you. Swim to the bank by going with the current but heading diagonally across the water. If you have friends still on the riverbank, try to get them to run ahead of you and throw the end of a rope into the water so they can pull you to safety. Swim on your back with

your feet out in front of you; that way, your feet rather than your head will hit rocks first. Think about where you can get out. Steep or muddy banks may be impossible to climb, so head for firmer, gentler landing points farther downstream. Try to grab any pieces of drift wood to give you further buoyancy.

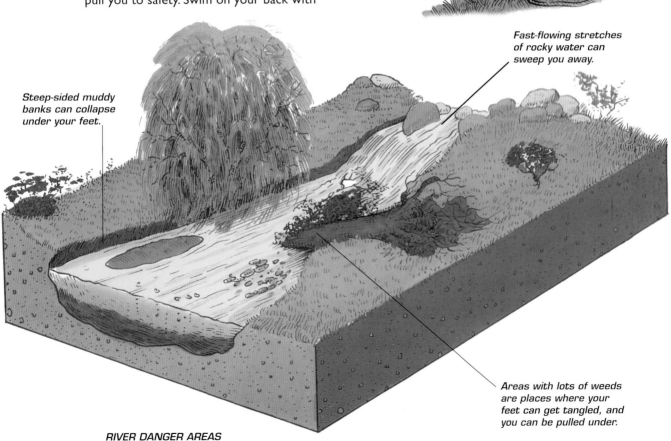

Fast-flowing stretches of rocky water can sweep you away.

Steep-sided muddy banks can collapse under your feet.

Areas with lots of weeds are places where your feet can get tangled, and you can be pulled under.

RIVER DANGER AREAS

TIP 67 Survive an Avalanche

Avalanches are awesome forces of nature. They can move faster than a speeding car and are powerful enough to rip up trees.

If you are walking in a mountainous area with lots of thick snow piled on the slopes and ridges above, be careful. If the snow sounds hollow underfoot, or if you can see cracks in it or hear rumbling, cracking sounds, get off the slope immediately to somewhere safe. If you see an avalanche rushing down at you, and you can't get out the way, pull off your backpack (and skis if you are wearing them), keep your mouth shut tight and your nose covered, and try to swim or roll with the rush of snow. Once you come to a stop, you may be buried and disoriented, and in complete pitch blackness. First, try not to panic. Clear away the snow immediately in front of your face to create a breathing space. To find out which way is up, push some spit out of your lips. The spit will travel downward either across your cheeks or fall directly away from you, so the opposite direction is the way to the surface. Start wriggling and "swimming" slowly to the surface, remembering not to panic.

TRUE LIFE SURVIVAL !

In June 1992, Colby Coombs, an outdoor adventure instructor in Alaska, discovered the terrifying power of an avalanche for himself. Coombs and two colleagues were on Mount Foraker when a storm created a huge avalanche that engulfed all three men and carried them 800ft (244m). The avalanche killed his two colleagues, but Coombs survived, though he had major injuries to his shoulder, spine, and ankle. Coombs knew he had to be tough to stay alive. Trying to ignore his pain, he traveled for several days through the wilderness, even making a dangerous 5-mile (8-km) crossing of the Kahiltna Glacier. He eventually reached help and safety, and today teaches classes in mountain safety.

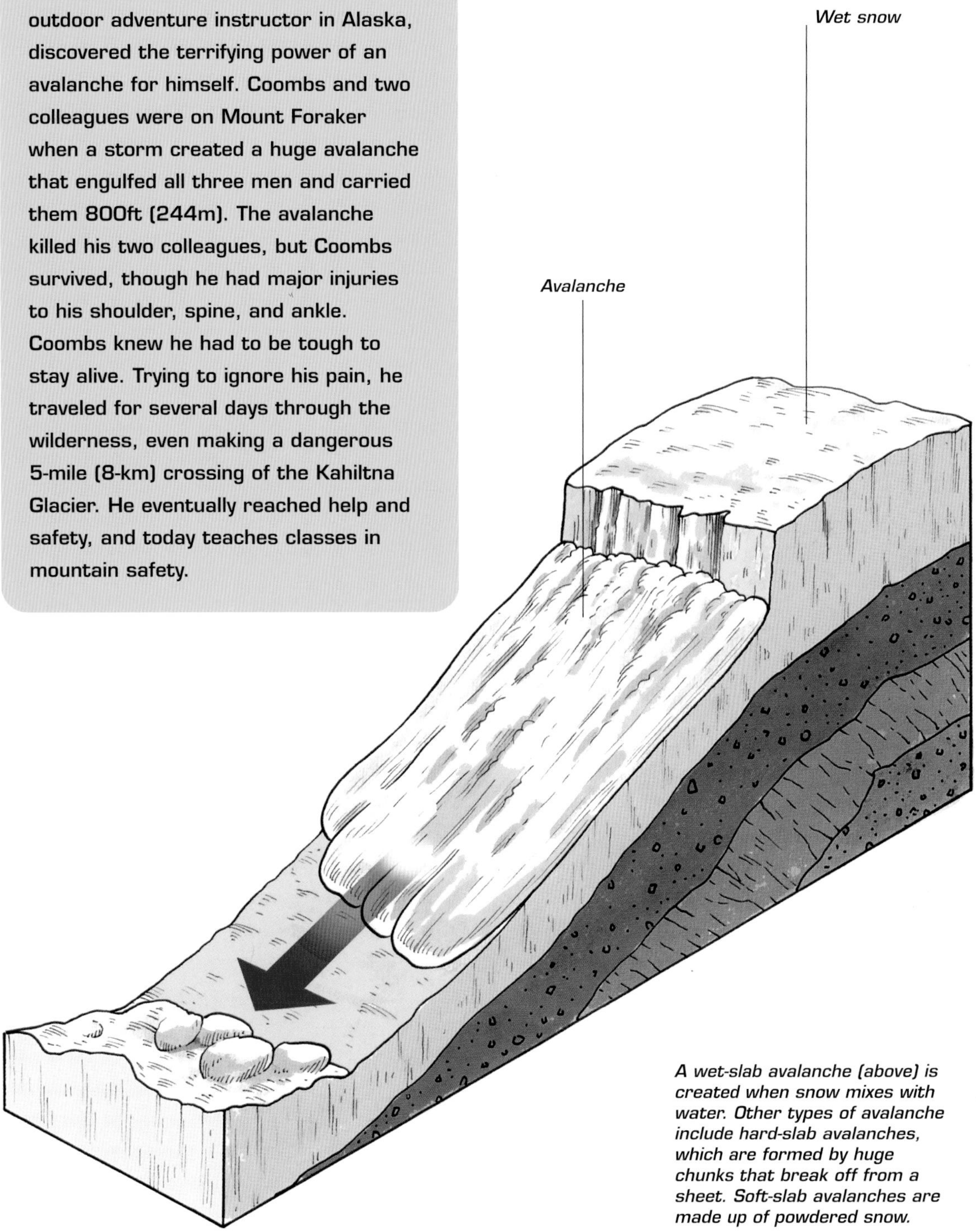

Wet snow

Avalanche

A wet-slab avalanche (above) is created when snow mixes with water. Other types of avalanche include hard-slab avalanches, which are formed by huge chunks that break off from a sheet. Soft-slab avalanches are made up of powdered snow.

TIP 68 Survive Falling into Quicksand and Bogs

The thought of falling into a sucking quicksand or bog is the stuff of nightmares. The wrong response will kill you.

The worst thing you can do if you fall into quicksand is to panic, struggle, and writhe, because this will make the quicksand drag you down even faster, and hold your limbs like cement. The first step to survival, therefore, is to relax your body as much as possible. Don't move around too much. Next, very slowly move your body to a floating position. Do this by angling your torso from side to side,

making a strong, slow swimming action with your arms until your body moves into a flat position on or near the surface of the quicksand. Whether you are now lying on your back or your front, start to crawl or swim your way to the edge of the quicksand, keeping your body as flat as possible to spread your weight. It will be exhausting, but you will eventually reach safety.

TIP 69

Survive Storm Conditions

In the wild, storms are out to kill you. Lightning crashes all around, and flying rocks and branches can hit you like bullets.

If lightning starts shooting down above you, crouch down very low—lightning is attracted to the highest object in an area, so make sure that it isn't you. For the same reason, don't try to find shelter under a tree or other tall structure, as the lightning might strike the tree and pass through to you. (Remember that lightning shocks can travel a long distance through soil and rock.) If you are carrying any long metal objects that can attract the lightning—such as radios with their antennae up or fishing rods—put them down and move away from them. Should you feel your hair suddenly stand on end, lightning might be about to strike. Throw yourself to the ground, preferably under shelter. To protect yourself from flying debris from the wind, crouch down behind shelter or in a trench or ditch. If you are caught in the open, pull your coat over your head to provide some degree of protection.

The most important thing to do in a storm is protect yourself from flying debris.

TIP 70 Survive the Heat

You have miles of desert to walk across, in scorching dry heat. Simple mistakes with clothing and fluids can cost you your life.

Extreme heat kills mainly by two methods—dehydration and what is called heatstroke. Dehydration means that your body is losing more fluid than it takes in—essentially, you are drying up. Heatstroke happens when your body seriously overheats. Both conditions can cause your brain and other vital organs to shut down. That's why you have two priorities in extreme heat: 1) to stay as cool as possible; 2) to take in as much fluid as possible. To stay cool, limit any movement to dawn and dusk when it is cooler, rather than trying to move during the blazing daytime temperatures. With a bright moon, you can also walk at night. Try to find shelter from direct sunlight because you will sweat less and therefore lose less body fluid. You can make a cool desert shelter out of two sheets of material with a gap between them (see illustration below)—this "roof" protects you from the worst of the sun's heat and sunburn. Increase your water intake as much as possible, and don't waste precious water washing yourself. If you have little water, avoid eating food as much as possible because digestion requires a lot of water, particularly for fatty foods and meats.

TRUE LIFE SURVIVAL !

In April 1994, Mauro Prosperi, a Sicilian athlete and policeman, began the Marathon des Sables, a competitive run across 145 miles (233km) of the Sahara Desert. During the run, a huge sandstorm struck, and Prosperi became hopelessly lost. He had only a small amount of water in his water bottle. In scorching heat, Prosperi stumbled on for mile after mile, being driven insane with thirst. He killed two bats he found in an old desert shrine and drank their blood, but then gave in to despair and tried to kill himself by slitting his wrists. He was so dehydrated, however, that the blood was extremely thick and wouldn't flow out properly. Prosperi staggered on, and eventually was found by a group of nomads on camels, who saved his life. He had walked for nine days and covered a grueling 130 miles (209km).

Another good way of getting out of the sun is to build an underground shelter. In desert conditions, it will provide excellent protection. Dig down about two feet (60cm) deep and create a space long enough to lie down in. Place two sheets or boards above the hole with an air space in between. The air space in the roof forms a layer of still air that will keep the shelter nice and cool. Be very careful making this shelter, however. Don't dig down too deep because, if the shelter collapsed on you, you might not be strong enough to dig your way out.

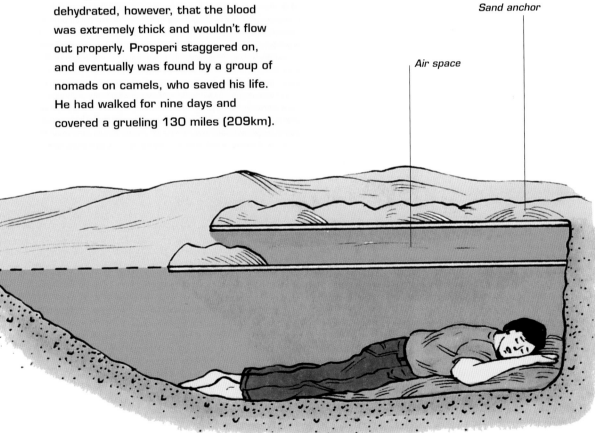

Sand anchor

Air space

TIP 71

Hot Weather Clothing

Even when a climate is baking hot, do not start peeling off your clothes to stay cool.

You may be hot, but it is still better to keep yourself covered with a long-sleeved shirt, pants, boots, and a wide-brimmed hat. The shirt and pants protect you from sunburn and insects, and trap sweat against your body (rather than let it simply evaporate away), and the hat shields your head and neck against overheating and your eyes from sunglare. The boots protect your feet against rough, hot ground and from the many dangerous animals that litter the ground. If you haven't got the correct clothing, you can make an Arab-style headdress from nothing more than a long piece of cloth tied around the top of your head. Make sure that this is long enough to cover the back of the neck—a long handkerchief hanging down from a baseball cap will do just as well. Tie another cloth over the lower half of your face to stop yourself from breathing in too much dust. A white sheet with a hole cut in the middle for your head will also make a cooling outer garment.

The baseball cap shields the scalp from the baking sun.

The neck shield is vital. Leaving your neck unprotected makes you more vulnerable to heat stroke.

The face protector stops you from breathing in dust and sand.

TIP 72

Survive the Cold

In Arctic temperatures, where even your breath freezes as it comes out of your mouth, how will you survive?

Cold kills. A condition called hypothermia strikes when the temperature at the core of the body drops below safe levels. Cold may also cause frostbite, when parts of the body freeze solid. To prevent both, wrap up very warmly—see Cold Weather Clothing (Tip 73) for more details. Stay as dry as possible. If you get wet, you will lose your body heat about twice as fast as when you are dry. Wind also makes the air temperature colder the faster it blows (this is known as the "windchill factor"). If you are caught in subzero conditions, like a blizzard, get into or make a shelter as quickly as possible. Huddle together with other people to share body warmth—don't be shy! Drink plenty of fluids because you can still get dehydrated in cold climates. Melt ice or snow before drinking it because sucking on frozen water will increase your loss of body heat. If you make a fire, make it on a bed of rocks so the fire doesn't melt surrounding snow and ice and extinguish itself. When you are out walking, don't wander onto frozen lakes and slip through the ice.

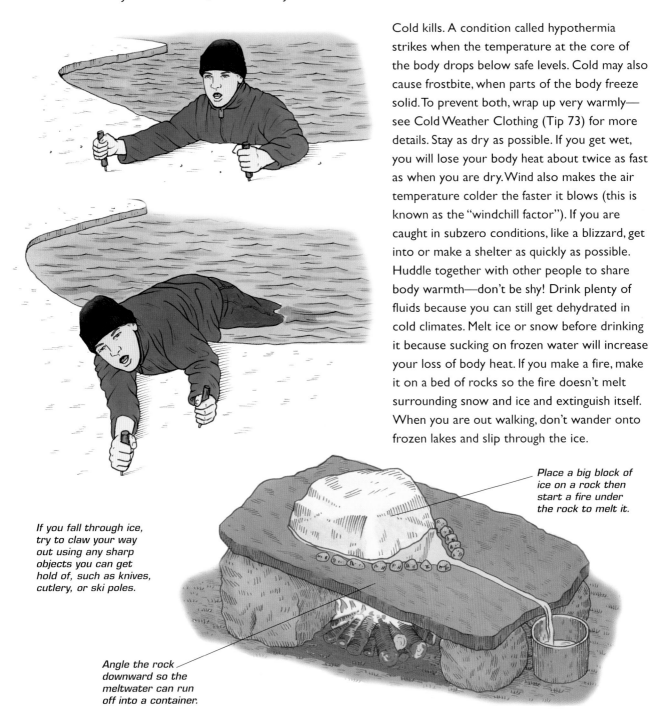

Place a big block of ice on a rock then start a fire under the rock to melt it.

If you fall through ice, try to claw your way out using any sharp objects you can get hold of, such as knives, cutlery, or ski poles.

Angle the rock downward so the meltwater can run off into a container.

TIP 73

Cold Weather Clothing

You are lost in a snowy wilderness, and night is approaching. As the temperatures plunge well below zero, it's probably only your clothing that will save you from from certain death.

In polar climates, make sure your head, hands, and feet are well covered—most of your body's warmth is lost through these areas, and these are all parts open to attack by frostbite. For the rest of your clothing, you should aim to wear plenty of thin layers with a windproof and insulated jacket over the top. Watch out for parts of your body going white, numb, and waxy. This is the early stage of frostbite. If your clothing isn't giving you enough protection, stuff it with some insulating material. Newspaper and straw are particularly good for this—bunch this up into loose bundles before stuffing it into your clothing. Also, any pieces of fur you've saved from hunting are obviously good protection. If any of your clothing becomes damaged in cold climates, repair it immediately with a needle and thread. Also, though you may be many miles away from a washing machine, do your very best to keep your clothing clean. Clothes that are covered with mud or dirt lose some of their insulating properties, meaning that they aren't as efficient at keeping you warm.

Full head protection

Insulated jacket

Mittens on cords so you don't lose them (never put gloves down in the snow)

Waterproof material

TIP 74

Make Sun or Snow Goggles

After hours under the winter sun, you may notice your eyes starting to burn and water. Act fast, or you'll be virtually blind in a few hours.

Bright sunlight or light reflecting off snow and ice can, over time, make your eyes horribly painful and they may also water. This may get so severe that you become blind. Though this will wear off later, it is obviously not good for your chances of survival. Luckily, there are a few easy ways to reduce the effects of light blindness. The easiest by far is to wear good sunglasses, but sometimes you don't have these with you. The first survival skill, therefore, is to rub a thick layer of black charcoal under each eye. You can get the charcoal from sticks that have been burnt until they turn black. (Let them cool down first.) Doing this stops some light from being reflected upward into your eye from the skin directly below. Better protection, however, comes by making a pair of goggles. Take a piece of thin cardboard, cloth, or even wood that is wide enough to fit across your face, and cut

two narrow slits for your eyes. Also, cut an indentation to fit over your nose. Next puncture a hole in each side and thread these with a piece of string that will go around the back of your head. These are your glasses. You may think that you look idiotic wearing them, and you will have a reduced field of vision, but they will do the job. If you happen to have a roll of camera film with you, this will also make good alternative eye protection.

TIP 75 Navigate by Dead Reckoning

If you've been walking for hours and don't know where you are, dead reckoning may get you back on track.

If you know your starting point on a map, a technique called dead reckoning will give you general idea about where you are after a few hours or a day of walking. It works like this. Before you set out on your adventure, measure out 328ft (100m) on flat ground. Walk down the track normally, counting how many steps it takes you to complete the distance. When you are out in the wilderness, keep a count of your steps in the back of your mind as you walk, putting a mark on a piece of paper for every 328ft (100m) traveled. Alongside this, keep track of your direction by using a compass, and mark on the paper every time you took a change in direction. With this information and using local landmarks, you can roughly plot your position on a map. Remember, however, that the length of your step changes with the terrain, so dead reckoning gives a general idea only.

Before setting out walking, always have a clear idea where you are headed. Fix your eyes on a clear, distant landmark and then use dead reckoning techniques to tell you how far you've traveled to reach that point. Track your journey on a map, and you will then have a good idea of how long other journeys will take.

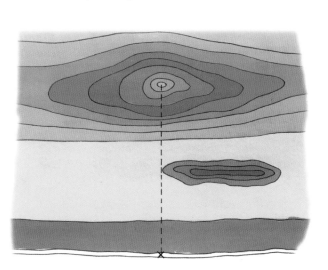

Navigate by the Sun or the Stars

For thousands of years, and across oceans and continents, people have been navigating by the sun and the stars.

Celestial bodies have been used for centuries for navigation. In the northern hemisphere, the North Star (also called Polaris) stands right over the North Pole, so you can use it to have a reliable idea of where north is. However, you can use any star in the sky to give you some idea of direction. Sit still in one place for 15–20 minutes and watch how a star moves in relation to a fixed object, say, a tree or mountaintop. If the star is rising, this means it is in the east; falling means it is in the west; left means it is in the north; and right means it is in the south. (The opposite is true for the southern hemisphere.) During the daytime, the sun is a useful navigational aid. Place a long stick in the ground and mark the tip of the shadow—this is your westerly point. After about 15 minutes the

shadow will have moved. Mark the tip of the shadow again—this is your easterly point. Draw a line in the earth between the two points to get an east–west line, then you will be able to draw a north–south line.

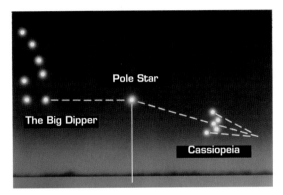

The Pole Star is a true guide to north and is set between the Big Dipper and Cassiopeia.

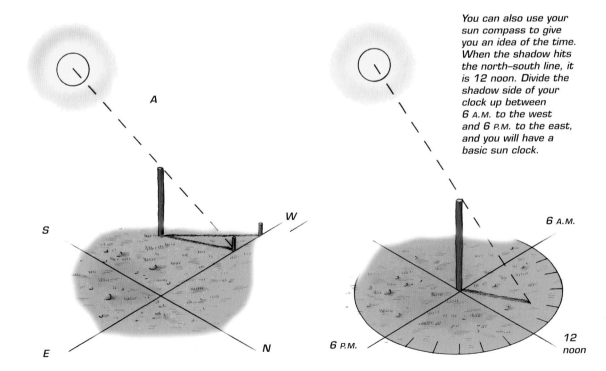

You can also use your sun compass to give you an idea of the time. When the shadow hits the north–south line, it is 12 noon. Divide the shadow side of your clock up between 6 A.M. to the west and 6 P.M. to the east, and you will have a basic sun clock.

TIP 77 Navigate by Nature and Landmarks

If you are lost, a bent tree or a patch of moss might not seem important—but it could get you home and save your life...

Using nature isn't the best way to navigate, but it can give you some clues about the direction in which you are headed. If you look at a map of the area you are going to, look at the direction in which the big rivers flow toward the sea, so when you come to these rivers they can show you where you are going. You can do the same with mountains or ridges, particularly because the sun will rise on the east side and set on the west. This type of navigation is even more simple near the coast—just remember which side the sea is on. Plants can also give you some clues about direction. Most plants love sunlight, so in the northern hemisphere they will often grow toward the south where the sun is strongest. The opposite is true of dark-loving plants like moss, which often prefer to grow on the sheltered north side of trees. Be careful, however, when navigating by nature because there can be lots of exceptions to the rules.

This tree has been pushed over by the prevailing wind (see arrow). If the winds generally come from the north, the tree will have fallen (roughly) to the south.

What can trees tell us? If moss is growing on one side, then that side probably faces north, away from the hottest southern sunshine.

TIP
78

Make Your Own Map

Making a survival map can be fun as well as practical. If you haven't got a professional map, producing your own will help you understand the terrain, steer clear of dangerous areas, and avoid getting lost.

The best method of making a map starts when you find a piece of high ground where you can see for a long way. Observe the terrain in front of you, and begin by drawing the largest features on a piece of paper—mountains, hills, tracks, rivers, areas of woodland, etc. Once you have plotted these down, start to fill in smaller, important details. Note where you can see potentially dangerous areas of terrain, such as steep slopes, or plot down any visible houses,

unusually high trees, or isolated outcrops of rocks. Write down your estimates of distances between major features—or, if this is too difficult, jot down an estimate of how long it would take to walk between those features. Finally, use your compass and draw compass points on the map. Your map may seem simple when you are up high, but when you are walking down in a forest or through a valley it can give you a real sense of where you are.

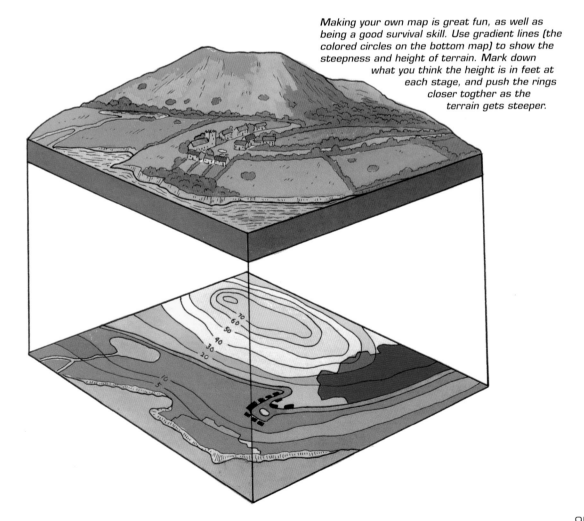

Making your own map is great fun, as well as being a good survival skill. Use gradient lines (the colored circles on the bottom map) to show the steepness and height of terrain. Mark down what you think the height is in feet at each stage, and push the rings closer togther as the terrain gets steeper.

TIP 79 Make Your Own Compass

Never head off into the wild without a good compass in your backpack. If you haven't got one, and emergency strikes, here's how you can make one with a few simple pieces of gear.

Any survival kit should contain a compass. A compass will help you to keep going in the right direction, and can prevent you getting lost in the wilderness. In an emergency, however, you can make an improvised compass. The essential ingredient of this device is a pin—you can use a sewing needle or pin, or any piece of thin, light metal, such as a paper clip. You have to magnetize the metal for it to work as a compass. Stroke the pin (a pin is best for the compass) with a magnet in one direction only—if you stroke toward the point, it will be the point that indicates north (A). If you don't

think you have a magnet, check for one inside any personal music headphones or rub the pin against a battery. If you really haven't got a magnet, stroke the pin with a piece of stone (B) or silk. This will produce a weak magnetic charge, but just enough for the compass. Once you have magnetized the pin, fill a nonmagnetic container (such as an aluminum or plastic cup) with water, then float the pin in the water on top of a leaf or piece of paper (C). Slowly, the pin will turn on the water to point north.

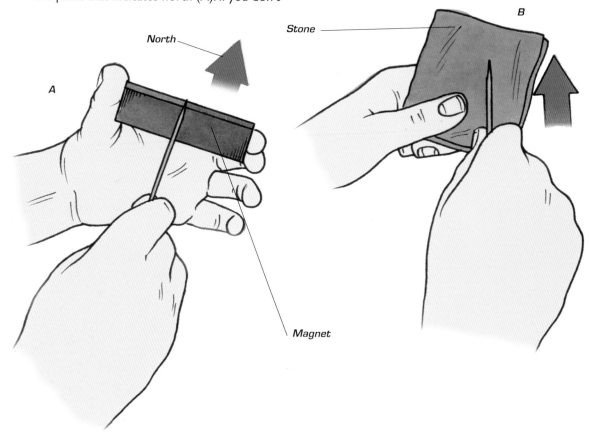

TRUE LIFE SURVIVAL !

Snowboarder Eric LeMarque showed amazing mental toughness when he was forced to survive in the Sierra Nevada mountains, in California, in 2003. He became lost while out boarding on the Mammoth Mountain, and found himself spending seven days and nights in the freezing wilderness. Though terribly frostbitten (his feet and parts of his legs later had to be amputated), he didn't give in. He made his own compass, ate pine seeds and tree bark for food, and correctly melted snow before drinking the water. He also used tree branches as bedding at night. The radio signal from his MP3 player helped to give him a sense of direction. All these measures let LeMarque avoid freezing to death and make it to safety.

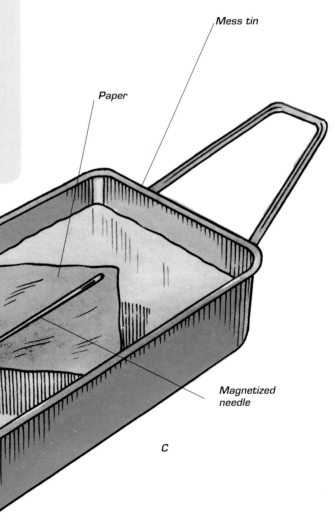

Mess tin

Paper

Magnetized needle

C

TIP 80 Travel Across Difficult Terrain

In treacherous terrain, one slip can send you slithering down a mountainside or tumbling into a river.

Walking through certain types of terrain is dangerous in itself, and a few basic tips can help you stay safe. In mountains, if the slopes are too steep to walk straight up comfortably, walk in a zigzag pattern up the slope, as this makes the angle less difficult (A). If you do walk straight up, turn your toes outward to provide a better grip (B). On rocky slopes, lower your weight gently, testing if the ground is crumbly and likely to give way under your foot. Never kick rocks—they may start to roll downhill and cause a landslide (C). When you are walking across large stones, test them before putting your weight down (D). They might look solid, but they could suddenly give way or slip from under you, resulting in a twisted ankle or a bad fall. If you have to move across snow and ice, take extreme care, especially on slopes. Should you fall and start to slide down the slope, dig in with your arms, feet, and hands to bring yourself to a stop—don't curl up in a ball (see opposite page). When walking in these conditions, kick your heel or toe into the snow before you put your weight down. A good idea is to link all members of your group together with a climbing rope, one behind the other (leaving enough distance to walk comfortably). The people behind the leader can use his or her footprints to make walking easier.

A

TRUE LIFE SURVIVAL !

In the wilderness, simple mistakes can kill you. That nearly happened to 87-year-old Allen Plumber in 2007, when he went out hunting with his faithful dog, Deb, in the Kisatchie National Forest, Louisiana. He had told people where he was going, but once out in the wilderness he changed his mind and went in a different direction. His compass didn't have its own light, which meant that when it became dark it was useless. He was also on his own—it is always better to stay with someone. The worst happened. He became lost and the weather turned into an icy storm. His body temperature started to plunge. Allen realized that he had to stay warm to survive, so he cuddled up close to his dog, sharing body warmth. After a while, however, he realized he had to move. He ended up crawling through the wilderness, and was eventually discovered and rescued.

If you do fall down a steep slope, you have to slow yourself down before you pick up too much speed. If you have an ice axe or ski pole, use that to help you (A). Dig the sharp point hard into the rock or ice and hang on until you come to a stop. Otherwise, spread your legs and arms outward, and dig your heels, toes, and hands into the slope (B).

B

TIP 81 Make Snowshoes

Trudging through deep snow will suck the energy out of your body and leave you prey to cold and exhaustion. Here's a solution.

Walking over deep snow can be incredibly tiring—after just a few hours, you will find that every step is exhausting. For this reason, try to make a pair of snowshoes. First you need some long pieces of wood and some rope or cord. One piece of wood should be longer than the rest—about 3–4ft (1–1.2m) long—and needs to be very flexible (A). A young sapling is good for this job. Sharpen the sapling to points at both ends (this will help the "heel" dig into the snow when walking) and trim all the pieces of wood of any spiky parts (B). Nylon cord is especially good for tying the shoe together because many other types of string will

become weakened once they are soaked by wet snow. Now bend and tie the long sapling into a oval shape to make the outer frame (C). Next, tie the other pieces of wood across the frame in a criss-cross pattern to make a platform for your boot (D). Finally, tie your boot directly onto the snowshoe, looping the cord around your toe, heel, and ankle in whatever way you can to make it stable, but leave some movement at the heel (E). Put padding under the rope around your ankle to prevent chafing. Repeat this whole process for the other foot to make the pair of snowshoes, and you should find walking much easier.

TIP 82 Crossing a River

Crossing a river is a moment of high danger. One slip in a strong current and you can be swept away.

To make a river crossing as safe as possible, first cut a long, strong branch that is at least as tall as you are. Then find a safe place to enter the water, with a long stretch of solid bank on the other side that isn't steeply sloped or too high to climb up. Ideally, cross the water where you can see that it is shallow, and avoid areas of water that move fast around rocks or swill around in circular currents. The best place to cross is often on the bend of a river, because if you slip you will hopefully be carried to a nearby bank. Keep your boots on, but take off your pants because these will be pulled by the currents. Enter the water with the stick stuck into the river floor upstream of you—the current will push it into the riverbed, and the stick will also partly break the flow of current against your legs. Lean into the current, and take slow shuffling steps across the river. Remember that the current will push you downstream as you walk, so pick your exit points diagonally opposite to your entry point. If you are in a group of three people, and you have a long rope, there's an even safer way to cross a river. First make the rope into a huge loop by tying the two ends together. Two people stay on the bank holding the loop while the third person crosses the river walking inside the loop, holding onto the rope at all times (A). Then the second person crosses (B), using the rope that is now stretched between the two banks. Finally, the third person crosses (C) in much the same way as the first person. The great thing about this technique is that if the person in the water slips, he already has hold of a rope and the people on the bank can pull him to shore.

TIP 83 Make a Log Raft

If crashing your way through thick jungle is exhausting you, there may be a better way to travel—on the river!

Making a log raft isn't easy. You start by laying two long, very strong poles down on the ground, parallel to each other and with a space in between. Next you need several logs, cut to the same length and with grooves cut near their ends. Now place the logs on top of the guide poles, seating the poles securely in the grooves. Then you need another two poles of the same dimensions and strength as the guide poles. These are laid across the top of the logs parallel to the bottom poles, and also set in

deep grooves. Once you have this basic structure, tie the ends of the top and bottom poles together extremely tightly, pulling the whole raft into shape and securing the logs together. For extra stability, put more lashings around the middle of the boat, and use whatever cord you have left over to tie any possible weak points together. Your log raft is now ready—just carve a paddle out of a long piece of wood and you are ready to test it on a shallow, safe stretch of water.

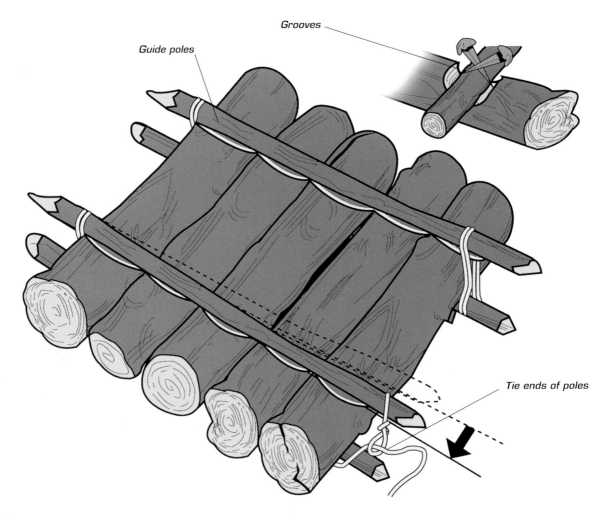

Grooves

Guide poles

Tie ends of poles

TIP 84

Make a Brush Raft

It's time to do some sailing with this quick and easy brush raft.

You won't be sailing across the seas in a brush raft, but you may be taking one down a river. The most important items in making a brush raft are one or two large, strong sheets of material, preferably a waterproof material like a groundsheet or tarp. Spread the smaller sheet out on the ground, and fill the middle with piles of vegetation—short sticks, reeds, twigs, and anything else that will float (A). Now tie two short, strong sticks together in a cross shape and place them on top of the vegetation. Using cord, tie the whole "parcel" together tightly (B). Then place this parcel in the middle of the larger sheet (if you have one—C). Wrap the larger sheet around it and tie it all tightly together with more cord (D). The brush raft is not large or stable enough for major adventures on the river, but it can be used for short journeys on quiet stretches of water. The best way to steer it is either with paddles or by using a long pole that you push down into the riverbed.

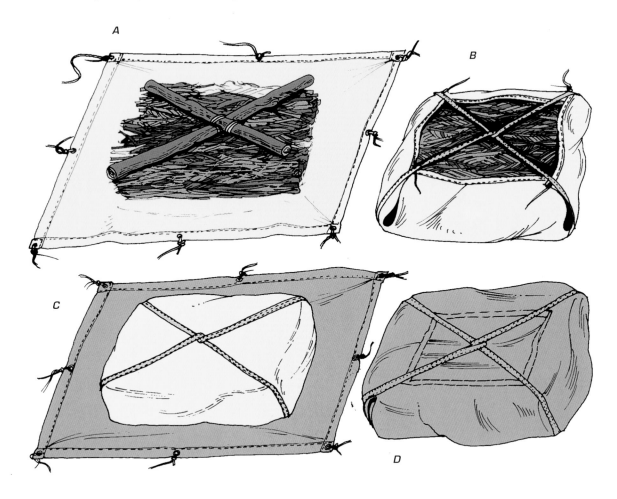

TIP 85 What to Do When Lost

When lost in lonely, harsh wilderness, you face two choices—look for help or stay where you are and wait for rescue.

You are already lost, so looking for help can be a risky business because you could become even more lost. As a general rule, you should head off for help only if one of your group is injured and needs urgent medical help, or if you are in a place where a rescue party is unlikely to find you. If you are in a group, stick together unless one of you is injured, in which case

someone should stay with the injured person. Before you leave to find rescue, preferably with a friend, write down on a scrap of paper any nearby landmarks that will lead the rescue party back to the injured person. When you set off, move downhill into valleys, try to find a river, and follow the river downstream—people tend to build habitations near rivers. If looking

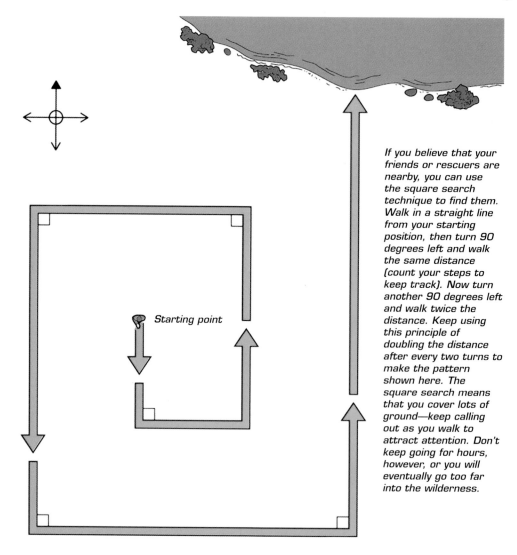

Starting point

If you believe that your friends or rescuers are nearby, you can use the square search technique to find them. Walk in a straight line from your starting position, then turn 90 degrees left and walk the same distance (count your steps to keep track). Now turn another 90 degrees left and walk twice the distance. Keep using this principle of doubling the distance after every two turns to make the pattern shown here. The square search means that you cover lots of ground—keep calling out as you walk to attract attention. Don't keep going for hours, however, or you will eventually go too far into the wilderness.

for rescue could make matters worse, wait for rescue to come to you. Use some of the signaling techniques described below to attract attention and move to ground where it is more likely that aircraft will be able to see you. As long as you told your parents or guardians where you were going (which you always should), a rescue party should find you.

TRUE LIFE SURVIVAL !

In 1971, German teenager Juliane Köpcke was the only survivor of a plane crash in the Peruvian jungle that killed 91 other passengers, including her mother. Alone in a frightening wilderness, she had a broken collarbone and was blinded in one eye, but her father had taught her a few jungle survival skills. She found a running stream and began to follow it downstream, hoping to find some habitation. The stream also gave her drinking water in the tropical temperatures. She eventually found an empty hunter's hut, where she found shelter and enough supplies to help her clean up some of her wounds. She survived for nine days in total in the jungle, and was eventually found and rescued by some loggers.

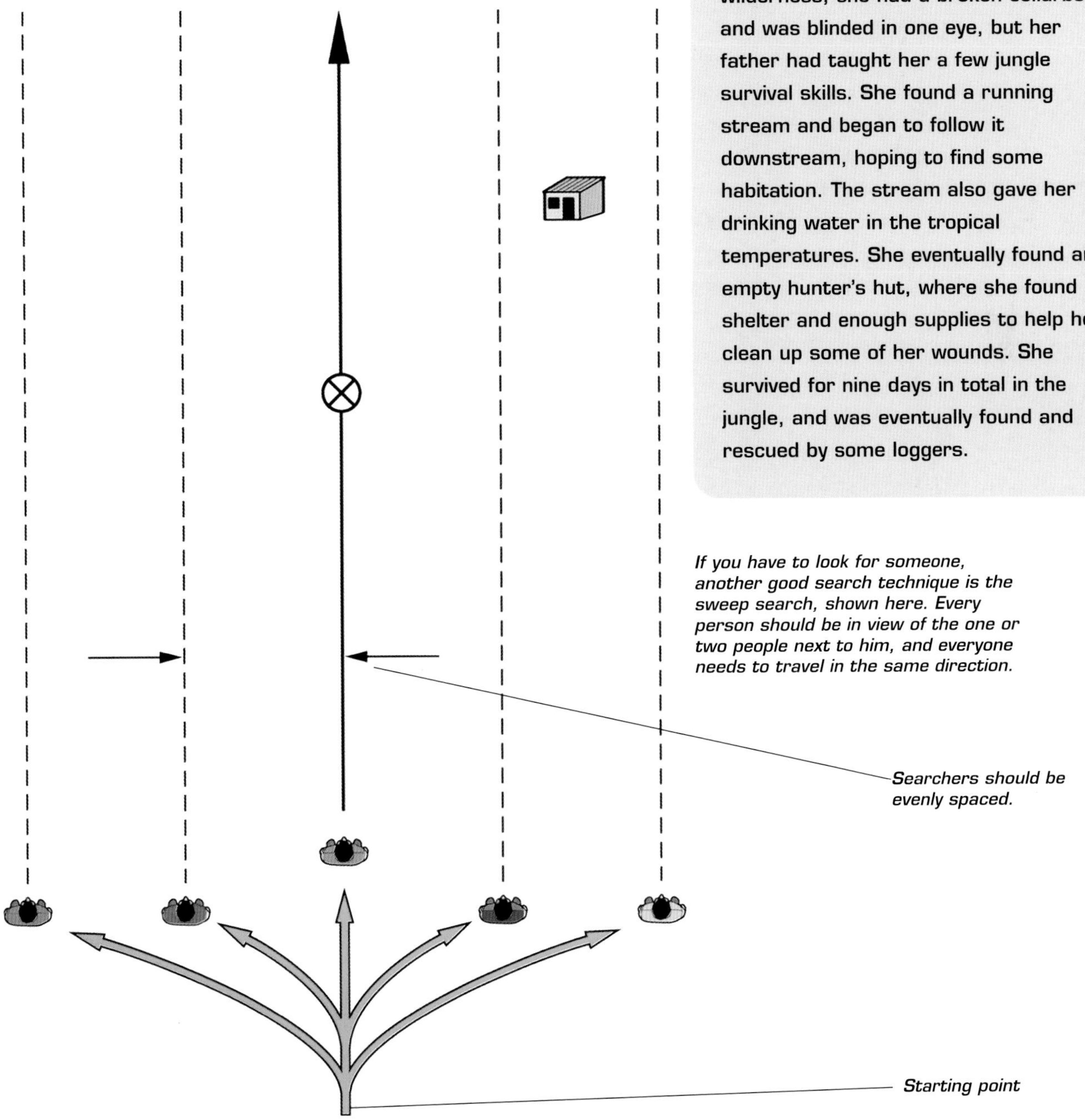

If you have to look for someone, another good search technique is the sweep search, shown here. Every person should be in view of the one or two people next to him, and everyone needs to travel in the same direction.

Searchers should be evenly spaced.

Starting point

TIP 86 Track People in the Wilderness

What do you do if one of your group goes suddenly missing in the wilderness? You use all your tracking skills to hunt him down.

First try to gain his attention by being noisy—that simply means shouting or blowing whistles. If he doesn't respond, you may have to attempt to track him down. To do so, start thinking like a detective. Ask yourself questions like: Where would he go? What is he thinking? Why would he go off? Answers to these questions may help you narrow the search down to specific areas. Next, like tracking animals (see Track Wild Animals, Tip 43), look for any sign of his movement—footprints, dropped items, broken foliage, etc.—and try to get an idea of his direction. If you are with other people, form a

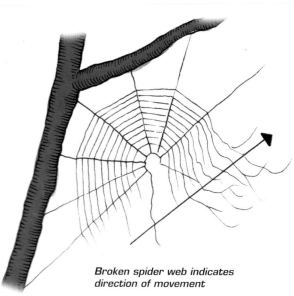

Broken spider web indicates direction of movement

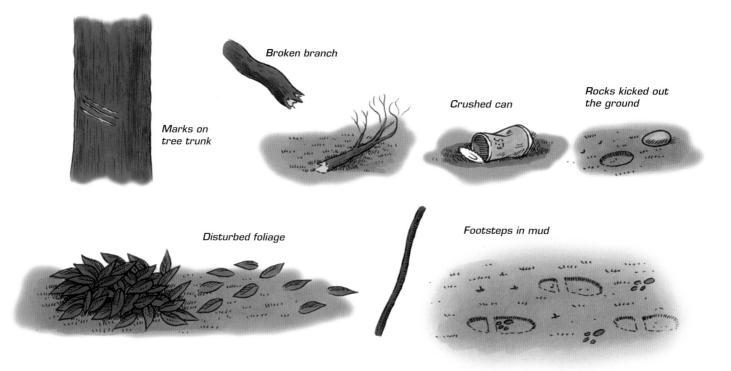

Broken branch

Marks on tree trunk

Crushed can

Rocks kicked out the ground

Disturbed foliage

Footsteps in mud

search party. Spread out in a wide line to make the search, walking in the same direction and keeping in view of each other so more of you don't get lost. When you turn, "hinge" on the person at either end so you don't cover the same ground again. Another type of search is the "square search." Start from the last position of the missing person, and work all the surrounding ground carefully, keeping all your senses alert for signs.

TRUE LIFE SURVIVAL

It helps to be a survival expert to stay alive in the wilderness, but toughness is just as important. In June 2003, an 11-year-old Cub Scout, Brennan Hawkins, went missing from a Scout Camp in a mountainous area in Utah. Despite a frantic search, there seemed to be no sign of the boy. He stayed missing for four days, and because he was such a young boy everyone feared the worst. Yet Brennan was alive. He managed to make some good decisions. He had a good method of keeping warm—he crouched on the ground, pulled his sweatshirt over his knees and tucked his head down, keeping as much body heat in as possible. He also made some bad decisions—he walked off into the wilderness, meaning that the rescue teams had a larger area over which they had to search. In the end, however, he was found, hungry, dehydrated, and sunburnt, but alive.

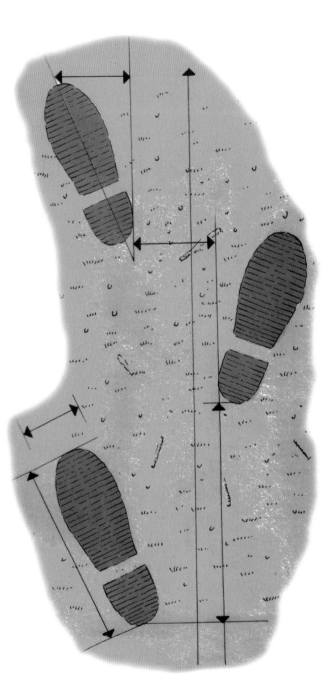

Remember that people often walk with their feet pointing outward. This means that if you are tracking footprints you shouldn't follow the direction of one footprint, but the direction between two or more footprints.

TIP 87 Predicting the Weather

In the wilderness, keep looking up. The skies will give you some big clues if there is dangerous weather on the way.

The most important weather predictions to make in the wild are when it will rain or snow—if you are not prepared, you'll be soaked or frozen. In terms of rain, look at the clouds. Signs of impending rain include: a very gray sky in the morning, which doesn't clear as the day goes on; fluffy clouds that are dark and flat at the bottom; huge, towering anvil-shaped clouds, which usually mean a storm is on the way. All these clouds are more likely to indicate rain if the wind speed is increasing, and if the temperatures are below zero snow could be on

its way. Nature has other indicators of bad weather. As the air moistens with the approaching rain, you may notice the following: curly hair getting curlier; pine cones closing up; grazing animals moving to lower land or lying down; bees heading back to their hives. Do not take these signs in isolation, but combined with basic weather-watching they should prepare you for the worst.

Watching plants is a perfect and effective way of predicting the weather. When plants flower, expect sunny weather; when they don't, rain will follow.

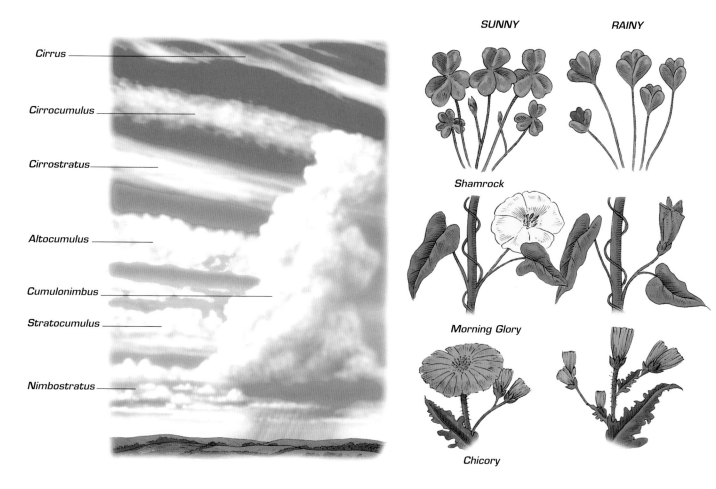

Cirrus

Cirrocumulus

Cirrostratus

Altocumulus

Cumulonimbus

Stratocumulus

Nimbostratus

SUNNY   **RAINY**

Shamrock

Morning Glory

Chicory

TIP 88

Make a Splint

Your friend has a shattered leg and you are miles from anywhere. How do you stop his injury from getting worse?

The purpose of a splint is to protect a damaged leg or arm from further harm while you are getting to a hospital or doctor. It is usually applied to broken limbs or limbs that have dislocated joints. To make a splint, you need one or two (preferably two) strong, straight "stabilizers," some material to act as padding, and some strips of material or cord to tie the splint on. The stabilizers can be anything that will keep the injury rigid, and can include ski poles, pieces of wood, branches, even rolled-up magazines or newspapers. First, get your friend to put his injured limb in the most comfortable position possible, lying down if he has an injured leg. Place the two stabilizers on either side of the injured limb, with some padding between them and the skin. Next bind the whole structure in place with the strips of cloth or cord, being careful not to move the break or dislocation as you do so. It extremely important that you do not cut off the blood flow to the limb by tying up the cloth ties too tightly. You can check by squeezing his fingernails or toe nails, and then letting go. If you don't see the red blood rushing back into the nail after you let go, loosen the ties a little.

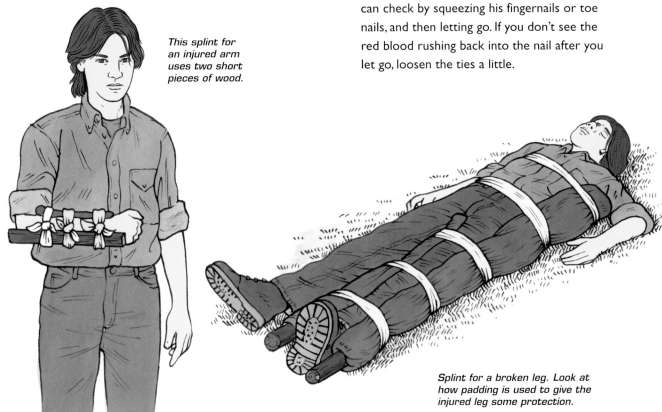

This splint for an injured arm uses two short pieces of wood.

Splint for a broken leg. Look at how padding is used to give the injured leg some protection.

TIP 89 Make a Stretcher

If someone is too injured to walk, and you can't get rescue to them, you might have to carry them on an improvised stretcher.

You can make a improvised stretcher out of just two long poles and some material to go between them. First, select two long straight branches (they should be slightly longer than the injured person); make sure they aren't too flexible. Or use stiff poles such as ski sticks or tent poles. If using branches, strip them of all protrusions using your knife. Now take a wide piece of material such as a blanket or tent groundsheet. Lay the poles at the edges on opposite sides, then start to roll up the sheet partway across until there is a strip left in the middle wide enough to accommodate him. It might actually be easier to place him on the blanket first before you start rolling up the edges. A group of four people can now lift up the stretcher using the padded poles. If you haven't got a big sheet of material, improvise using either empty backpacks or jackets—reverse the sleeves inside the body of the jacket, then push the poles through the sleeves (see illustration below).

TRUE LIFE SURVIVAL

Sometimes the human body can perform amazing acts of survival all on its own. On October 7, 2006, Mitsutaka Uchikoshi went hiking in Mount Rokko, near Kobe, in Japan. He was with others at first, but he left them to go back down the mountain on his own. Unfortunately, he fell down a cliff and hurt his back. He was completely unable to move and he feared that he would simply freeze to death on the mountain. Then a strange thing happened. He slipped into what doctors later described as a state of "hibernation." His body temperature, heart rate, and breathing all dropped very low, and he went into a trancelike state. He survived in that way for 24 days without anything to eat or drink. He was eventually discovered, and even though he was seriously ill he went on to make a full recovery.

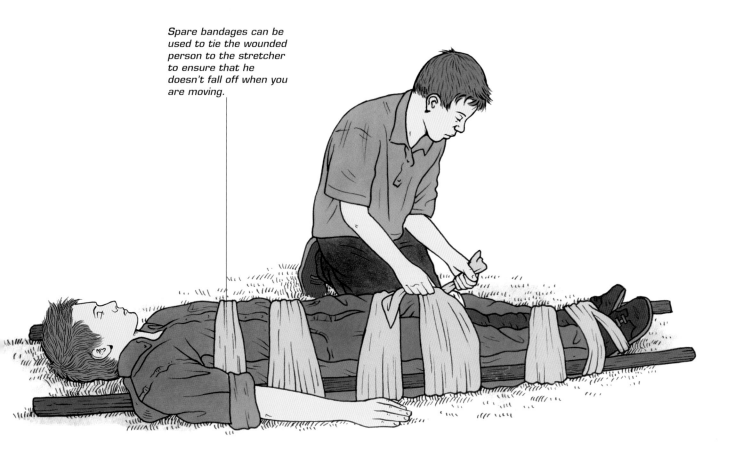

Spare bandages can be used to tie the wounded person to the stretcher to ensure that he doesn't fall off when you are moving.

TIP 90 Make Crutches

Hobbling across the wilderness with an injured leg is agony, but you can make the journey easier with these homemade crutches.

Improvised crutches require some care to make properly, but you can do it with just two forked branches from a tree. The branches need to be strong and their total length needs to be just longer than the distance between the injured person's armpit and the ground. Strip off any small branches (A), then bore two holes across from each other in the fork— these are for the handgrips—and cut down the tops of the fork to fit into the armpit piece (B). Cut the armpit pieces and the handgrips down as shown below, and try to make them fit into the sockets as tightly as possible (C), even if it means hammering them into place (D). Putting some sticky tree resin into the holes before fitting can strengthen the fit and ensure durability. The crutches are nearly done, but you will need to wrap the armpit pieces with plenty of cloth (E) to make sure that they fit comfortably into the armpits without rubbing them too much. Improvised crutches won't stand up to too much heavy use, but they could help someone with a sprained ankle to keep moving.

TIP 91 Bandage a Wound

You might have stopped the bleeding, but in the wild any wound can become infected and dangerous if you don't look after it.

The main aim with any flesh wound (A) is to stop the bleeding (see "Treat a Cut," Tip 94). Once you have the bleeding under control, you need to bandage the injury. First clean the wound as much as possible (wash your hands before you do this). Pick specks of dirt out of the wound with tweezers and clean it with water, but stop this immediately if the wound starts bleeding again. Now take a clean pad of material and a bandage (B). Bandage the pad directly into place (C), with the pad over the injury. If you don't have professional bandages,

use strips of any material available, but make sure that they are totally clean (boiling them in water for a few minutes will sterilize them). After bandaging the pad, stick the ends of the bandage down with tape or a pin, or simply tie them in place. As with all bandages, don't tie too tightly or you will cut off the blood circulation to the limb. If you find blood still seeping through, apply pressure with your hand to the place where the blood is coming from (D) until it seems to stop. Then put another pad on top of the bandage and tie that in place (E and F).

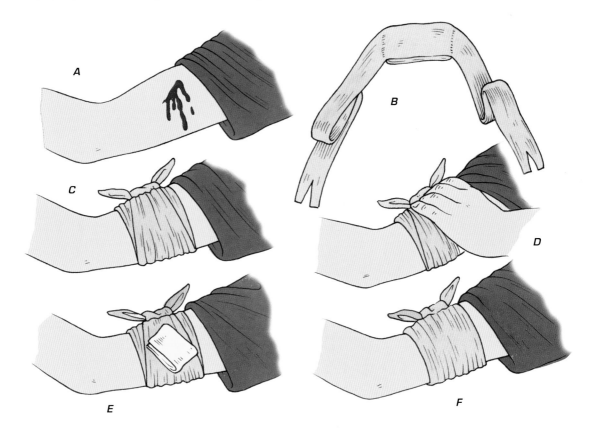

TIP 92 Stitch a Wound

Stitching a wound is not recommended for anyone who is not a medical professional. But if there is almost no chance of rescue, you may not have much of choice.

Stitching is mainly for clean, straight-cut wounds. Never attempt to close up a ragged, dirty wound or one that is more than 12 hours old. To do the stitching, you need a needle and thread, both of them boiled in water for 10–20 minutes to make them sterile (free from germs). The wound needs to be cleaned, so wash your hands carefully with soap (if you have it), making sure you remove dirt from under your nails. You can now make the first stitch. At the midpoint of the injury, push the needle and thread through both sides of the wound in the way shown, then tie the ends of the thread together and tie them off to pull the open skin together. Repeat this process on either side of the center stitch as many times as required to bring the whole wound neatly together. Remove the stitches 5–10 days afterward by snipping them and gently pulling out the thread. However, if the wound shows signs of infection—oozing puss, a bad smell, bleeding—they may have to be removed early and the wound cleaned out before restitching.

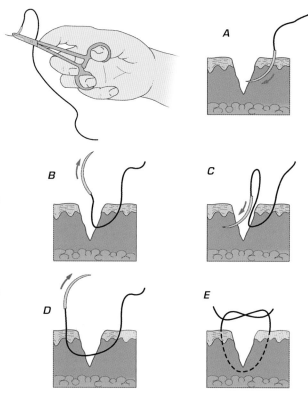

TRUE LIFE SURVIVAL !

Bill Jeracki, a 38-year-old doctor, had to make what must be one of the toughest decisions ever. In October 1993, he was out fishing in a remote part of Colorado when a huge boulder crashed down onto his leg, crushing and trapping him. Jeracki's situation was made worse by the fact that he was wearing only thin clothing and a snow storm was on its way for the night. He knew that he had to free himself, or he would freeze to death. His solution was unbelievable. Using only his pocket knife, Jeracki actually sawed through his own leg, cutting it off at the knee and freeing himself. He crawled to his car and then drove with one leg to a nearby town, where he was taken by helicopter to a nearby hospital. Few people could do what Jeracki had done, but he did live to survive another day.

TIP 93

Treat a Blister

We've all had blisters. In a survival situation, however, they can slow you down and stop you from reaching safety quickly if you don't treat them.

Blisters tend to appear on the feet or the palms of the hands, and are caused by things such as boots and ropes rubbing against the skin. If a blister develops, the general rule is to leave it alone. Picking at it with your nails is a good way to make the blister infected, so resist the temptation. If the blister is large and painful, and you can't rest to let it heal, you may have to lance it (burst it) with a needle. First clean the area around the blister with soap and water. Then sterilize a needle by boiling it in water for 10 minutes or holding it over a flame (let it cool before using it). Push the needle slowly into the outer edge of the blister (A), remove the needle, and let the fluid ooze out, squeezing the blister gently with a clean pad (B). Once it has emptied, leave the blister skin where it is and cover the blister with a bandage (C).

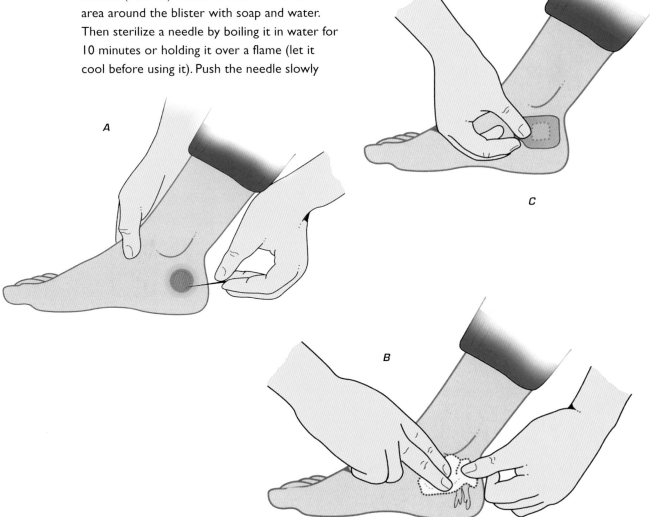

TIP 94 Treat a Cut

When blood is pumping out of an injury, take a deep breath, don't panic, and put your first aid skills into action.

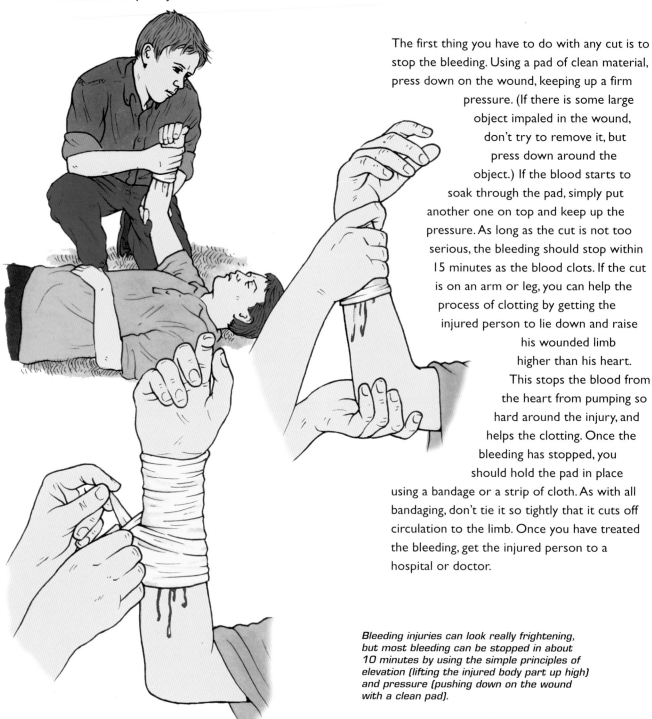

The first thing you have to do with any cut is to stop the bleeding. Using a pad of clean material, press down on the wound, keeping up a firm pressure. (If there is some large object impaled in the wound, don't try to remove it, but press down around the object.) If the blood starts to soak through the pad, simply put another one on top and keep up the pressure. As long as the cut is not too serious, the bleeding should stop within 15 minutes as the blood clots. If the cut is on an arm or leg, you can help the process of clotting by getting the injured person to lie down and raise his wounded limb higher than his heart. This stops the blood from the heart from pumping so hard around the injury, and helps the clotting. Once the bleeding has stopped, you should hold the pad in place using a bandage or a strip of cloth. As with all bandaging, don't tie it so tightly that it cuts off circulation to the limb. Once you have treated the bleeding, get the injured person to a hospital or doctor.

Bleeding injuries can look really frightening, but most bleeding can be stopped in about 10 minutes by using the simple principles of elevation (lifting the injured body part up high) and pressure (pushing down on the wound with a clean pad).

TIP 95

Treat Sunburn

However tough you are, never underestimate the sun. Exposing your skin to hot sun for hours on end can result in some horrible burns.

A sunburn not only increases the risk of dangerous conditions such as heatstroke, but scientists have also discovered that it can be a factor behind skin cancer later in life. The two main ways of preventing a sunburn are: 1) to cover up with clothing, which means pants and long-sleeved shirts and a broad-brimmed hat; 2) to apply a good sunscreen, with an SPF of at least 30, before going out in the sun. If you do get a sunburn, however, you need to cool down the area as much as possible. Put cold compresses—pads of material soaked in cold water—on the burned area, refreshing the cold water every time the pad gets warmed through. If you are so badly sunburned that your skin has blistered, don't pop the blisters. Any burn uses up body fluid to heal itself, so make sure you drink plenty of water to keep hydrated. Cover up and stay out of the sun while your sunburn heals, but remember that it is best to prevent getting a sunburn in the first place.

Staying in the shade and covering up with clothing are the best ways of preventing sunburn.

If someone has a severe sunburn, and they seem very confused, hot, and unwell, their condition could be life-threatening. Get them into the shade, wrap them in a sheet and soak the sheet with cold water to cool them down. Call a doctor immediately.

TIP 96

Treat Bites and Stings

You are deep in the jungle or a summertime forest. Whatever you do, the insects are going to treat you as a meal or a target.

The general treatment for insect bites is to leave them to heal by themselves. Avoid scratching them and apply some antihistamine ointment. An antihistamine is a medicine that reduces swelling, and can be bought from a drugstore—it is a good idea to take a tube of antihistamine cream with you out into the wilderness. Bee, wasp, and hornet stings can be more of a problem because the stinger is often left stuck into your skin, where it continues to pump out poison. To remove the stinger, try to grip it with tweezers below the poison sac at the end and pull it out. If you squeeze the poison sac itself, the sting will get worse. Once the stinger is removed, place a pad of material soaked in cold water on top of the sore skin. The cold material will help reduce swelling, which is the main reason why a sting continues to hurt and throb. If you walk through grassy areas with bare legs, you might find that a tick has lodged itself into your skin. Ticks lock into your skin with strong jaws. Using tweezers, grip the head as close to the skin as possible and work the tick out. Do not just pull on the body, because it will snap off, leaving the jaws inside you to cause infection.

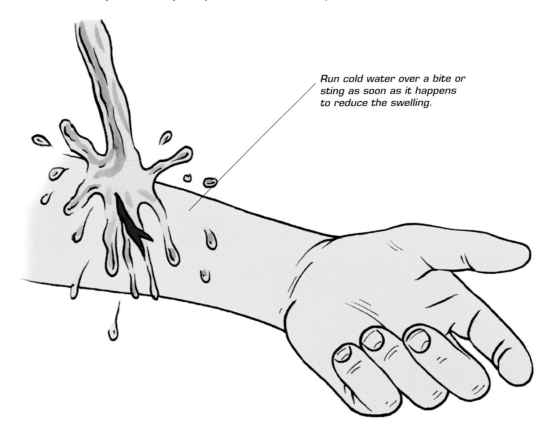

Run cold water over a bite or sting as soon as it happens to reduce the swelling.

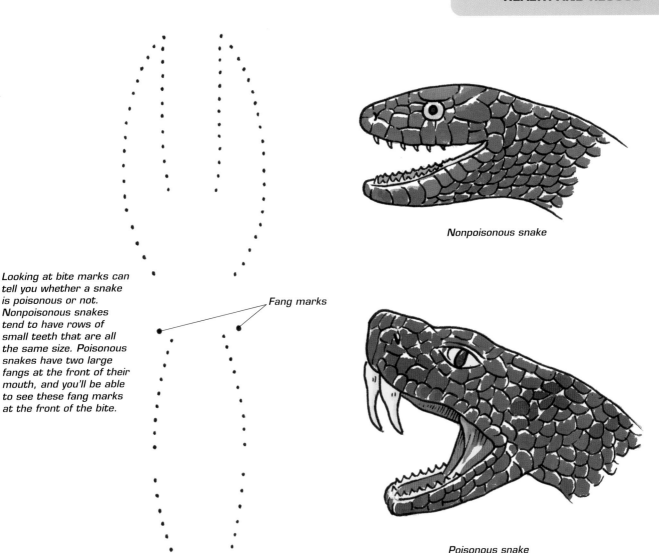

Nonpoisonous snake

Looking at bite marks can tell you whether a snake is poisonous or not. Nonpoisonous snakes tend to have rows of small teeth that are all the same size. Poisonous snakes have two large fangs at the front of their mouth, and you'll be able to see these fang marks at the front of the bite.

Fang marks

Poisonous snake

TRUE LIFE SURVIVAL

One of the most aggressive insects in the world is the Africanized Honey Bee. In June 2007, a 61-year-old man and his grandson were out hunting quail near Wickenberg, Arizona. They were suddenly attacked by a ferocious cloud of honey bees, which seemed intent on killing them. They sprinted to their truck a few hundred yards away, but even when they were inside the truck there were about 200 bees in there with them. They fought the bees for about half an hour in the truck, before finally escaping in a passing vehicle that took them to the nearest hospital. In total, the man received more than 70 stings and the boy had more than 50, and they were very lucky to have survived the attack.

TIP 97 Signal Using Light

If a rescue party can't see you, they can't rescue you. Here's how you make yourself visible for miles around.

In survival, signaling means drawing attention to yourself so rescue parties can find you. There are three methods of signaling with light— artificial light (such as that made by flashlights), fire, and sunlight. The first is the easiest to do. If you have a flashlight and it is nighttime, flash your torch in the SOS pattern three times (see Use Morse Code, Tip 99). Don't, however, do this so often that you exhaust your batteries in just a few minutes. Instead, do it at quarter-hour or half-hour intervals, and try to point the light from high ground toward different parts of

Catch the sun's rays with a small mirror and flash them out at passing ships, planes, or people. Angle the mirror directly toward your target.

the landscape and skyline. Fire can be used to signal in daytime and nighttime. Make a smoky fire during the day by adding lots of green twigs, damp grasses, or pieces of rubber (vehicle tires are great) and at night use dry, fresh wood to make a bright blaze. Build the fire on high ground to increase the chances of it being seen. Finally, during the daytime use a mirror, a piece of bright metal, or the back of a CD/DVD to reflect sunlight out toward aircraft, boats, or rescuers. In bright sunlight, this signal can be seen more than 60 miles (100km) away. If possible, try to flash out the SOS signal.

TRUE LIFE SURVIVAL !

In January 2003, Ken Hildebrand was out on his quad bike checking some animal traps in a remote wilderness area, when his bike turned over and trapped his legs, injuring him seriously. He would stay like that for the next 96 hours in freezing conditions, but he used some excellent survival skills to see him through. First, he covered himself with a beaver carcass to keep warm, and he used another carcass as a pillow. Second, he licked at frost on the grass to give himself some fluids, even though he was very dehydrated by the time he was rescued. Finally, he used some orange tape to make a big "X" on the ground, to make himself easier to spot by search aircraft. In the end, he was discovered by a man out hiking with his dog, and taken to safety.

TIP **98** Signal Using Sound

A search party is nearby, but you are hidden from view in a deep, dark forest. Now it's time to get noisy.

Noise travels a long way in many wilderness areas, particularly deserts and mountains and especially in dry, calm conditions. (Wind and rain can dampen or carry away sound.) It is a good way of signaling if you are in an area where it is hard to see you, such as a forest, but you should try to get to high ground before making the noise because thick foliage also limits the distance sounds travel. The most basic sound signal is a shout, which is more effective if several of you do it at the same time and in the same direction. However, the noise of whistles carries much farther. An international distress signal for use with a whistle is six long blasts followed by six short blasts. Leave a minute of silence between each sequence of sounds. The same can be used for a hand-held foghorn, though you are unlikely to be carrying one of these.

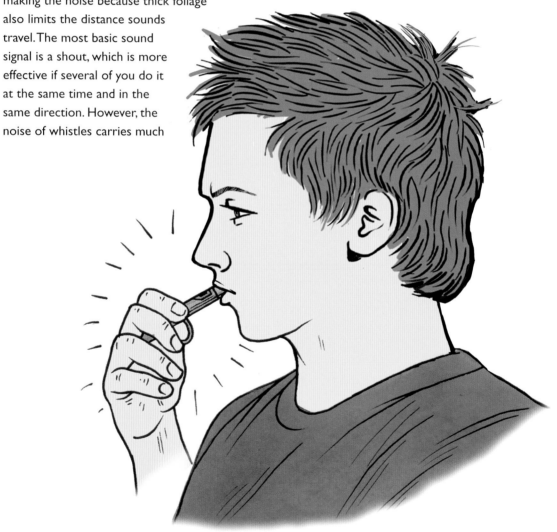

Use Morse Code

Morse Code has been used for more than 160 years, and it could still help you survive in today's wilderness. You can become a survival communications expert yourself by mastering Morse Code.

Morse code was first developed back in the 1830s as a general form of communication, but it has been vital for people in survival situations ever since. The system consists of different combinations of dots and dashes for each letter of the alphabet and the numbers 0 to 9. These dots and dashes can be transmitted to other people by using sound, light, or electronic means, the dots representing short notes while the dashes represent long notes. You can transmit Morse Code by whistle, flashlight, flashing mirror, or radio keypad, and its great advantage is that you can tell people exactly what the problem is. Learn all the Morse Code symbols here, or write them down on a piece of paper and carry them with you. If you remember just one sequence, remember the international "SOS" distress signal: three short signals, three long, then three short. With any Morse message, remember to leave a short gap between each letter or number sequence so that they don't get mixed up.

A .—	M ——	Y —.——
B —...	N —.	Z ——.. —
C —.—.	O ———	1 .————
D —..	P .——.	2 ..———
E .	Q ——.—	3 ...——
F ..—.	R .—.	4 ....—
G ——.	S ...	5 .....
H	T —	6 —....
I ..	U ..—	7 ——...
J .———	V ...—	8 ———..
K —.—	W .——	9 ————.
L .—..	X —..—	0 —————

TIP 100 Sending a Radio Message

In a life-or-death situation, one of your best pieces of equipment may be your cell phone or radio. One call and help could be on its way...

If you are well prepared for a survival emergency, you will have gone into the wilderness with a survival radio and, better still, a cell phone. Don't think a cell phone will make you safe in the wilderness, however, as many cells can't pick up reception in remote areas. VHF radios, however, can work anywhere, but try to get to high ground to make a transmission because landscape features can block their signals. The international Mayday channel on a radio is Channel 16. Press the

transmitter and clearly state: "Mayday. Mayday." then give your name, situation, and your best description of where you are. Make the transmission clear and short, then release the transmitter button and listen for any response. Repeat the message at regular intervals, but don't use up your batteries too quickly—set a schedule of every quarter or half hour, with two transmissions each time. Remember, don't call Mayday unless you are seriously in trouble, because the rescue services will go into action.

VHF radio

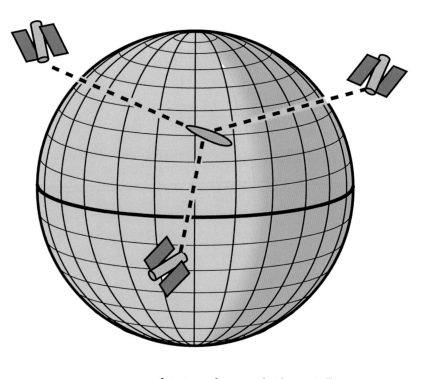

A system of communications satellites encircle the globe. With a cell phone you can use this system to call for help from remote areas. If you are traveling abroad, however, make sure your cell phone is set up to make foreign calls.

Make Ground-to-Air Signals

Want to be seen by a rescue aircraft flying thousands of feet up in the air? You can be with these easy-to-make ground-to-air signals.

Today's rescue services frequently use aircraft in their wilderness rescue operations because they can cover huge areas of ground in a short space of time. The problem is that one or two people on the ground are often hard to see in the landscape from hundreds of feet up. That's where ground-to-air signals come in. These are large signs you make on the ground from whatever materials are available, and which stand out clearly when viewed from the sky. The diagram here shows you the list of international ground-to-air signals. You can make these out of anything—clothes (especially brightly colored ones), sleeping bags, branches, earth, piles of snow, or piles of leaves—but there are a few general rules to follow. Make the signs big—up to 33ft (10m) long is good. Ideally, build them from material that contrasts with the ground—such as green branches on bare brown earth—or pile the materials high to throw large shadows that are very visible. Place the signals in flat, open areas where they can be more easily seen from the air, such as high ground. Finally, make sure that you arrange for the signs to be removed once you have been rescued, or change the sign to a direction arrow (No. 9) if you move to another location.

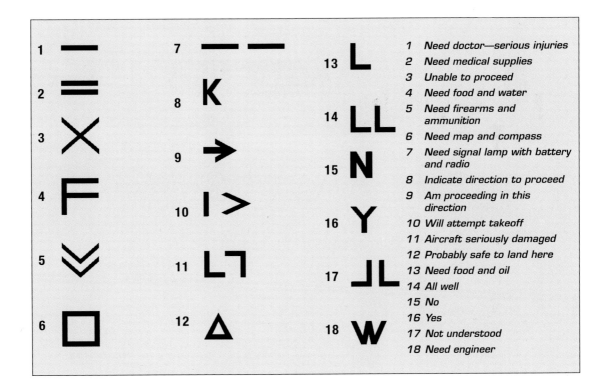

1. Need doctor—serious injuries
2. Need medical supplies
3. Unable to proceed
4. Need food and water
5. Need firearms and ammunition
6. Need map and compass
7. Need signal lamp with battery and radio
8. Indicate direction to proceed
9. Am proceeding in this direction
10. Will attempt takeoff
11. Aircraft seriously damaged
12. Probably safe to land here
13. Need food and oil
14. All well
15. No
16. Yes
17. Not understood
18. Need engineer